I0091657

# Living in Death

# Thinking from Elsewhere

*Series Editors*
Clara Han, Johns Hopkins University
Bhrigupati Singh, Ashoka University and Brown University
Andrew Brandel, Harvard University

International Advisory Board
Roma Chatterji, University of Delhi
Veena Das, Johns Hopkins University
Robert Desjarlais, Sarah Lawrence College
Harri Englund, Cambridge University
Didier Fassin, Institute for Advanced Study, Princeton
Angela Garcia, Stanford University
Junko Kitanaka, Keio University
Eduardo Kohn, McGill University
Heonik Kwon, Cambridge University
Michael Lambek, University of Toronto
Deepak Mehta, Ashoka University, Sonepat
Amira Mittermaier, University of Toronto
Sameena Mulla, Emory University
Marjorie Murray, Pontificia Universidad Católica de Chile
Young-Gyung Paik, Jeju National University
Sarah Pinto, Tufts University
Michael Puett, Harvard University
Fiona Ross, University of Cape Town
Lisa Stevenson, McGill University

# LIVING IN DEATH

*Genocide and Its Functionaries*

RICHARD RECHTMAN

Translated by Lindsay Turner

Foreword by Veena Das

FORDHAM UNIVERSITY PRESS
New York 2022

This book was originally published in French as Richard Rechtman, *La vie ordinaire des génocidaires*. Copyright © 2020 CNRS Editions.

Cet ouvrage a bénéficié du soutien des Programmes d'aide à la publication de l'Institut Français.

This work, published as part of a program of aid for publication, received support from the Institut Français.

This work received the French Voices Award for excellence in publication and translation. French Voices is a program created and funded by the French Embassy in the United States and FACE Foundation (French American Cultural Exchange). French Voices Logo designed by Serge Bloch.

Fordham University Press gratefully acknowledges financial assistance and support provided for the translation of this book by the École des hautes études en sciences sociales (EHESS), the labex TEPSIS, and CESPRA.

L'ÉCOLE des hautes études en sciences sociales   tepsis   CESPRA

Copyright © 2022 Fordham University Press

All rights reserved. No part of this publication may be reproduced, stored in a retrieval system, or transmitted in any form or by any means—electronic, mechanical, photocopy, recording, or any other—except for brief quotations in printed reviews, without the prior permission of the publisher.

Fordham University Press has no responsibility for the persistence or accuracy of URLs for external or third-party Internet websites referred to in this publication and does not guarantee that any content on such websites is, or will remain, accurate or appropriate.

Fordham University Press also publishes its books in a variety of electronic formats. Some content that appears in print may not be available in electronic books.

Visit us online at www.fordhampress.com.

Library of Congress Cataloging-in-Publication Data

Names: Rechtman, Richard, author. | Turner, Lindsay, translator. | Das, Veena, writer of foreword.
Title: Living in death : genocide and its functionaries / Richard Rechtman ; translated by Lindsay Turner ; foreword by Veena Das.
Other titles: Vie ordinaire des génocidaires. English
Description: New York : Fordham University Press, 2022. | Series: Thinking from elsewhere | "This book was originally published in French as Richard Rechtman, La vie ordinaire des génocidaires. Copyright © 2020 CNRS Editions"—TItle page verso. | Includes bibliographical references.
Identifiers: LCCN 2021037935 | ISBN 9780823297856 (hardback) | ISBN 9780823297863 (paperback) | ISBN 9780823297870 (epub)
Subjects: LCSH: Genocide—Psychological aspects. | Mass murderers—Psychology.
Classification: LCC HV6322.7 .R4313 2020 | DDC 364.15/1—dc23
LC record available at https://lccn.loc.gov/2021037935

Printed in the United States of America

24 23 22   5 4 3 2 1

First edition

# CONTENTS

# FOREWORD

VEENA DAS

As I hold this book in my hands, I have the feeling of a work that is both passionate and subtle. Written with inexhaustible tact and compassion, it asks how to render the experiences of those who had become simultaneously perpetrators, victims, survivors, and witnesses of the killing machines that are evoked by such names as Rwanda, Bosnia, Cambodia, Nazi Germany. Do these places bear any relation to names such as My Lai, Hiroshima, Nagasaki, Palestine, Kashmir that theories of international relations or theories of jurisprudence of genocidal violence scrupulously exclude from their understanding of genocide? Richard Rechtman is not interested in refining the classifications underlying such questions as to which kinds of war are just—regrettable but necessary, as much liberal theory will have it—or, whether particular religions or ideologies generate the potential for greater or lesser violence; nor does he place himself as a moral judge, not at least until he has been able to arrive at some understanding of how it is that ordinary men, any men (and perhaps women given the right circumstances), could become part of modern killing machines, part of the administration of death.

One has to listen closely to what Rechtman is saying, for sometimes his expressions are so ordinary, so devoid of drama, that one's attention might slip. For instance, let us listen closely to his words when he says, "This book does not set out to add anything to existing analyses of the ideological conditions leading to the implementation and practice (especially) of mass extermination. That is not my objective here. After having spent more than thirty years studying genocide and its victims—from an anthropological perspective as well as in my role as a psychiatrist—it is increasingly clear to me that it is not ideologies that kill, but men." So stark, so simple. But, what kind of men? The answer, or at least the beginning of an answer, is an unsentimental formulation culled from years of immersion in the stories of survivors of the Cambodian genocide among whom Rechtman worked as a psychiatrist in a public hospital in Paris, and from the court room testimony of the head of the S-21 prison camp in Phnom Penh, known popularly by the name of Duch. Rechtman has ploughed through the archives of the S-21 prison camp and, most tellingly, through the testimonies of the ordinary civilians, which provided "an unprecedented set of materials relating to the quotidian reality of the genocidal regime" in Cambodia. From these documents, he sees a different kind of reality emerging than the one portrayed by questions such as whether the men who participated in this whole apparatus of the killing machine were monsters, or were they perhaps ordinary men? Did they have any choice? Instead, Rechtman reads in these testimonies, and in the memories of the survivors he came to know as a psychiatrist, the traces of a form of life that became the quotidian reality of the Cambodian people on whichever side of the divide they found themselves in—the pure or the impure, the loyalists or the traitor-enemies, the innocent or the guilty. Are we right, then, to think of the period of the genocide as having generated "a form of *life*"? Does a form of life contain in itself the seeds of generating brutal deaths? With no hope of doing full justice to this compelling book for which I cannot find adequate adjectives, I will indicate the way Rechtman overturns the questions we habitually ask of such events as genocides from within the disciplinary frameworks of anthropology, psychology, or political philosophy. The vocabulary that emerges in Rechtman's discussion draws from the traces of pervasive death he found in the testimonies of survivors he treated in Paris as well as from legal testimonies in court trials. His words take us to a different register of theorization on the ordinary within the scenes of destruction. Let me say how this book reorients our thinking.

First, Rechtman offers the idea of the ordinary life of the executioners implicated in mass killing almost in defiance of the notions of the banality of evil through which Arendt characterized the legal trial of Eichmann and her understanding of totalitarianism. The ordinariness that Arendt evokes in the case of Eichmann had such a powerful impact on social theory only because of the hold of the idea in the first place that someone to have actively planned mass killings at such a scale must have been a monster. However, as Rechtman says, it is not Eichmann's being *ordinary* that could explain his participation in the mass executions. Instead of being caught in the snares of the question as to whether there are any special characteristics of those who participate in projects of mass killing versus those who resist them, Rechtman argues that we should be looking at the overall organization, the industrial nature of the killings, and what being captured in this killing machine did to the ordinary life of the killers. In other words, from the dominant models of the tripartite structure embedded in the distinction between perpetrators, victims, and witnesses, Rechtman shifts the emphasis to ask, what was the everyday life of those recruited in the project of administration of death on a mass scale?

The results of this shift of questions are surprising. Based on his perusal of the archive of legal and administrative documents and his clinical experience with the survivors and with the "petit" executioners, Rechtman finds that the focus of their narration was, in fact, not on the act of killing but on the preparatory work, the calibration of details, the meeting of targets, and the sensory experiences of the smell of blood, or removal of bodies and the sheer exhaustion of the work they had to perform. Did this exhaustion and the endless repetition of classifying, killing, removing bodies, and cleaning up the blood completely obliterate any other feelings the killers might have had for these very same people who they might have known in their previous existence as neighbors, kin, friends, co-workers? Most work on genocide that theorizes on the neighborhood in the context of mass violence asks how neighbors could kill each other. That is, indeed, a good question but with few good answers. The shift in this question that Rechtman makes, asking, what kind of feelings define the projects of killing for the killers, yields completely new insights. And no wonder that the emotions he finds in the testimonies of the "petit" executioners are disgust, fear, and exhaustion. Not grief, not guilt, not shame, not remorse—in fact, none of the emotions that high moral theory would make us look for.

Second, Rechtman's book creates a new way of thinking in moral philosophy. Much discussion on genocide ends up with a test question about self-knowledge: "In those circumstances, would I have become an Eichmann or a Duch, the chief executioner of Pol Pot? Would I have been able to resist the pressures of the regime in power?" Rechtman's genius lies again in shifting the question and asking what accounts for the availability of so many ordinary men to become the hands and feet of the killing machines. He provides a meticulous account of how the systems of classification worked to sort out the so-called natives and the "new people" who were supposed to have lost their connections to the soil because of their education, elite status, or western influences. But those who were the "petit" executioners, the small cogs in the machine despite being the ones who did the work of killing were not that far from the subjectivities of the victims. Both were surrounded by the physical presence of death, not its shadows, but its physicality. The killers knew only too well the cost of not only defiance and resistance but also of small failures in meeting targets or slipping into complete exhaustion.

The great philosopher Stanley Cavell thought of horror as the possibility of the dissolution of human identity, or, one might say, the dissolution of our identity as human. As Cavell said, memorably to my ears, only of the human can we say that it is capable of the inhuman. Rechtman understands this insight well as he shows that there is no single moment in which the transformation of the human into the inhuman happens. Instead, there are these slow movements made up of countless details that we should be looking for if we want to understand the horror that the dissolution of one's identity as human entails.

The third important point that comes out in the text is the infirmities of the judicial reasoning behind declarations of mass killing as genocide. The debates on these issues are not new, but most discussions have been around the difficulties of ascertaining responsibility and culpability. International or national tribunals on genocide have resulted in the trials of very few leaders in mass killings. These trials are important but leave many issues unresolved. In the case of Cambodia, it took forty years before (only) three leaders were indicted: first for crimes against humanity, and then, for the crime of genocide. Rechtman shows how the judicial definitions of what constitutes a population in a genocide enables judicial processes to bear on racially or ethnically defined populations that have been subjected to extermination; but this same definition excludes from its purview, say, Stalinist or Maoist purges (for instance) that were more driven by class warfare than ethnic or racial enmities. While no easy answers are available about how to redefine the crime of genocide to include mass exterminations on the basis of class warfare, or for revolutionary justice, Rechtman demonstrates how our thinking on crimes against humanity or genocide is still heavily marked by the Nazi experience, which limits our ability to take other experiences of mass violence into account.

Finally, Rechtman makes a very important contribution to consideration of what constitutes an ethnography of violence. Violence is not treated here as a spectacle but as routinized (though not normalized) within the everyday. I think the very texture of the writing, which is more on the minimalist side as far as ethnographic examples or case descriptions are concerned will stimulate a lot of discussion on the idea of what is an example, what is a detail, or what is an instantiation. Said otherwise, we cannot say in advance whether a single word or phrase will open up a whole world that reveals its alterity or closeness to our own worlds, much as a detail in a painting can unravel the sense of its overall composition; or else if we will need to show multiple layers through which a description is secured, much as we might rake layers of fallen leaves for a patch of ground to be revealed to our eyes. Although these issues are not directly addressed in the book, the emphasis on forms of life, and the potential of forms of dying contained within these forms, leads to new questions about method, and about rigid or flexible ontologies, for further conversations.

The measured conversations with current French social theory and psychoanalysis that Rechtman engages in demonstrate how a certain Eurocentric conceit comes to mark classical theories of violence, cruelty, and horror. This book is unique in being able to provide an archaeology and anthropology of the specificity of the Cambodian case but it is also a stunning contribution toward rethinking all contemporary forms of violence, from war to genocides to terrorism, dismantling the edifices of current political theorizing that is so dependent on the distinction between state and non-state actors, civilized violence of "just wars," and barbaric violence attributed to groups defined as "terrorist" or "jihadi," or simply engaged in spasmodic rather than consistent violence driven by rational considerations. Current psychological theory, in its turn, seems obsessed with the subjective life of the mass killers and executioners, as if violence has made it permissible for us to imagine that we can see the perpetrators as if they were made of glass through and through.

I find it important to say that Rechtman nowhere forecloses the possibility that the terms of analysis and description he offers—"forms of life," "everyday," "descent into the ordinary," "our life in language," and "the inhuman as an eventuality of the human"—could be woven into other kinds of questions. For instance, we could ask how those who inherited these memories might weave them over time into the inheritance of other pasts such as is now becoming evident in the recreation of Buddhism in Cambodia, or, on making those who died ghostly deaths into ancestors through rituals of *dana* and of passing on one's good karmas for reclaiming those lost to kinship. Survivors might again begin to touch on issues of guilt and survival through still different vocabularies such as those of *karma*, reincarnation, *dharma*, *dana*, that were made to disappear in the genocidal purges. But just as the Eurocentric conceit that Rechtman critiques so correctly cannot be put aside in any further developments on theories of violence, so some easy access to tradition cannot be assumed in any descriptions that attend to the question of how to rebuild life on ruins that are specific to *this* society of *this* time.

The words from this book that will stay forever with me are the simple depiction: "But the quotidian reality of those who kill is first and foremost dominated by the physical presence of death and its residues, which structure the substance of each day. It is not their sadism that

drives them to live in a universe where it is omnipresent, physically and spiritually, but their quotidian life
that leads them to spend the majority of their days with
it. In Cambodia during the Khmer Rouge period, or in
Rwanda during the Tutsi genocide—as in most places
where mass atrocities are committed—genocidaires share
this corporeal presence with their victims. They live and
they evolve in this corrupted universe. Bodies are present
in their conversations; they pollute the water and the soil,
working their way eventually into the food supply. And
while the act of killing is ultimately so easy for these
people, the constant presence of human remains, on the
other hand, is more difficult. It becomes the daily stuff of
their conversations, their jokes, their frustrations, and
their weariness."

The task before us is to ask how we allow ourselves to
be educated by this hard labor Richard Rechtman, the
anthropologist, the psychoanalyst, the novelist, has per-
formed on our behalf and for us.

# Living in Death

# INTRODUCTION

Today there exists a substantial catalog of stories and confessions from individuals who have participated in mass murder: spontaneous testimonies, interviews with researchers and documentarians, and minutes from the trials where these men and women were heard. Attentive reading of such evidence reveals that there are many more similarities between the different actors—for example, between a Khmer Rouge executioner, a Serbian nationalist during the conflict in the former Yugoslavia, a Hutu extremist in the Rwandan Tutsi genocide, a member of Bashar al-Assad's special forces who participates in gassing civilian populations, and even an Islamic State fighter—than between the ideologies in the names of which these actors kill.

Comparing different practices of genocide on an empirical level has the advantage of putting into perspective the modes of organization and execution of massacres that are very similar in numerous ways—very often independent of the specific nature of the deadly ideologies that order them. Indeed, the political or juridical classifications of the crimes (genocides, mass killings, extremist violence, or even major terrorist acts, such as the September 11 U.S. attacks or the 2015–16 attacks that shook Paris and Brussels) are themselves not enough to account for the nature of commitment on the part of the men and women who carried them out.

This question of comparison and classification is not new. Following the events of September 11, 2001, at the opening of the international conference on extremist violence that took place in Paris on the 29th and 30th of November, 2001, political scientist Jacques Sémelin emphasized that current events had brutally overtaken the discussions that had been prepared long in advance.[1] Fewer than three months after the attacks that bloodied the United States and rocked the order of the world, the question of whether these acts fell under the category of "classic" terrorism, acts of war, or civilian massacres that occur under extreme genocidal regimes became pressing. The principal contributions published the following year in the *Revue Internationale des Sciences Sociales* endeavored to respond to this question, at least partially, attempting a sociological explanation of the problem of extreme violence.

The classificatory system for different types of massacres that Sémelin proposed,[2] which would be refined in his work *Purify and Destroy*,[3] rests primarily on a principle of distinction based on the intentions of those who organize massacres. Sémelin designates two main models—each of which have several subcategories—that are distinguished according to the ultimate goal of the responsible authorities: to destroy in order to subdue, or to destroy in order to eradicate. This is an essential distinction. The point of Sémelin's analysis is to allow a rational comparison between mass atrocities, however horrific they might be. Any other approach, which would attempt to rank massacres according to the degree of atrocity committed, would risk being not only deeply ethnocentric and historically dated—it would be strictly dependent on whatever was seen as the pinnacle of atrocity at a given era and in a particular cultural context—but above all would be quite weak heuristically because levels of violence are likely to fluctuate so much over the course of a single conflict.

From a political science point of view, the advantage of Sémelin's theory is that it permits comparison between massacres based on politics and general ambitions. In this way, it is a kind of institutional analysis; it focuses on the measures put into place by totalitarian regimes to achieve their ends. In the case of "destruction for submission," massacres force civilian populations to bend to the order established by armed forces, either loyalist or rebel. Mass executions are intended to put populations in line, to quell attempts at sedition, and to punish potentially resistant civilians. The number of lives lost is less important than the order these repressive regimes seek to impose. Here massacres accompany and serve repressive politics. In the case of "destruction for eradication," on the other hand, the main objective is radical purification—the total physical elimination of the population in question. Genocide, of course, represents the archetype of this model, in which extermination as such is an objective of war.

Yet on the level of the men who participate in these crimes, Sémelin's distinctions appear less useful. If we look closer, we realize that the intentions of planners and commanders have little effect on how the massacres are carried out. Those who kill act in the same way regardless of whether the goal is eradication or submission. In other words, across the ends of purification, destruction, punishment, subjugation, and extermination, the modalities for administering death differ little.

In order, then, to analyze processes of mass extermination beginning neither from politics nor from the ideologies (or religions) that seem to motivate them, but instead from the point of view of the men who carry out these crimes, it seems to me necessary to keep in mind five factors common to all situations where massacres constitute the heart of an administration of death. These factors are: the asymmetry between perpetrators and victims, the military strategy that operates to assure elimination, the planning of crimes, the territories concerned, and finally the recruitment of killers. By "administration of death," I mean a global politics not only in which putting to death a segment of the population is among the principal instruments of social control (regardless of the final intention), but also in which the administrative management of the whole of the population is structured around the death of some.

Looking at these five parameters in more detail, we notice first of all that there is always an asymmetrical relationship between the perpetrators—usually armed forces—and the victims, unarmed civilians. At a far remove from the classic context of combat, military strategy is limited to selecting victims and then gathering them in places favorable to mass killings: a village square, a church—like at Oradour-sur-Glane, or in Rwanda—a clearing, or a field in which pits for graves have perhaps already been dug. The choice of victims corresponds to a preexisting division between the pure and the impure, the latter necessarily destined for death. The targets are thus not chosen for what they represent—as is the case with classical terrorism, whose targets are strongly symbolic (police, politicians, heads of state, and so on)—but for what they are. In other words, individuals are found guilty of being what they are: impure Muslims, Jews, traitors, and so on, who "deserve" on that account to be executed. The third factor, to that end, is that massacres are prepared according to a precise organization that makes possible both the minute planning of objectives— thanks especially to propaganda diffused through "official" channels to justify the crimes—and the quest for the greatest yield, or the choice of means of execution likely to guarantee the greatest "productivity."

These first three factors are joined by the demarcation of territory concerned. And finally, there is the recruitment of killers (ordinary military forces, police forces, militias, or even single individuals). Those recruited are not necessarily the most motivated or convinced; they are simply those who are the most readily available. Of the five, this final factor is certainly the most contested. It is what animates the majority of contemporary controversies surrounding the phenomena of enlistment, radicalization, fanaticism, and the final act of killing itself. But these are not simply examples of adherence to a "cause." On the contrary, the most available individuals are of all kinds: ideologues, psychopaths, delinquents, or ex-convicts, of course, but also so-called *ordinary people*.

The most ideologically fervent, of course, would seem to be the most obvious candidates for recruitment; it is no accident that propaganda aims specifically at those who might already be considered indoctrinated. But, in fact, nothing is less certain. If we compare massacres, it becomes apparent that the most ideological individuals are rarely the ones who put the quotidian work of killing into motion. It is true that these individuals do form a vast network of sympathizers, propagandists, possible accomplices, smugglers, and other protectors. They are sometimes likely to offer shelter or to guard arms caches. But most often their participation is limited simply to expressing sympathy for extremist theses; with the exception of certain lower-ranking officers, they are rarely killers themselves. This division of tasks exists everywhere, from among the Khmer Rouge to direct executioners during the Holocaust (the *Einsatzgruppen*,[4] for example, or the camp guards) to Hutu assassins, and so on. In other words, those likely to become mass killers are not recruited exclusively from the ranks of the most ideological. The majority of these killers have no more personal or ideological motive than they do passion for death or for murder, such that they have no need to liberate any sadistic impulses in order to kill. They kill just as simply as others go to work.

This book does not set out to add anything to existing analyses of the ideological conditions leading to the implementation and practice (especially) of mass extermination. That is not my objective here. After having spent more than thirty years studying genocide and its victims—from an anthropological perspective as well as in my role as a psychiatrist—it is increasingly clear to me that it is not ideologies that kill, but men. And men, it seems, are all too ready to take up arms whatever their motivating convictions. This book is exclusively and entirely concerned with these individuals—not with their beliefs, not with their certainty that some people are superior to others, and not with the necessity, according to them, of purifying the world by exterminating those they simply no longer wish to hear about.

This reflection originated at the very beginning of my clinical and anthropological practice, which started at the transit center in the Parisian suburb of Créteil, where

I was recruited in 1987 to handle psychiatric consultations. This center received all the refugees from Southeast Asia arriving in France before they were sent across the country. This work continued in my involvement with the Association de Santé Mentale (Mental Health Association) of Paris's 13th arrondissement—this arrondissement's public psychiatry sector—where an aid and research program centered on the psychiatric issues of refugees from Southeast Asia was created in 1990. The aims of this program were to offer consultations to the neighborhood population—more than 15,000 refugees, 60 percent from Cambodia—in their languages, to guide them through public institutions according to their needs, and to supplement the whole through research work in the community itself. Close analysis of the stories of refugees and former torturers, as well as regular listening of their sufferings, allowed for a different understanding of what happened in Cambodia between 1975 and 1979. By plunging into their daily universe, so to speak—from their symptoms, dreams, and ordinary fears to the uncertainties of their memories—it seemed to me possible to return to the nature of criminal intention, to reveal its inner workings from its consequences. What we undertook was a kind of archaeology of genocidal intentionality starting from the traces left in the stories of survivors—in their behavior, their comportment, in what they said and sometimes did not say, in what they had experienced.

I pursued this "archaeological work" for many years, even if I did not consciously know what it was I was doing—especially because the term "archaeology" imposed itself only later, at the moment I realized that death saturated all the stories told to me, the symptoms that my patients presented and the impressions I felt in contact with them. These traces translated not only each individual story, but also by their recurrence indicated a collective history, the thread of which could only be followed outside of any clinical explanation. This was the method I adopted from the beginning of my practice. I continued it working with victims of other massacres in the following years, and again more recently in investigations with survivors of Syrian state repression, as well as Afghan victims of Taliban and Islamic State violence, and finally in the cases of young people incarcerated in France after their return from Syria. In other words, my investigations centered on the men and women directly implicated, starting from their everyday reality, much more than the organizational and ideological structures of which the majority were the victims and others made the instruments.

For too long, it was believed to be possible to explain killers' behavior starting from the ideologies they held—and yet not all of them were committed ideologues. Many had never read a single line of propaganda, which seemed in their eyes too tedious. Most understood only the rudiments of the rhetoric of the "beauty of purification." And yet they killed, more or less passionately, more or less enthusiastically, sometimes with cynicism or sadism, but rarely with remorse. For some, this meant docile submission, following orders to the letter. For others, it meant anticipating these orders for the sake of good standing. Others constantly sought ways to do as little as possible in order to stave off fatigue. It has long been wondered who these men and women capable of such rote killing were. Did it weigh on their consciences? Did they not sense the horror of their acts? Did they have no compassion for their victims? Did they never realize they were killing their fellows in cold blood? Or were they anesthetized? Did they find themselves in an altered state of consciousness, suspending all moral judgment? Or were they simply bloodthirsty monsters, stripped of all humanity?

Whether they give orders or merely serve minor roles, it is now customary that the perpetrators of mass massacres should be considered "ordinary men." In other words, they are seen to be men and women who do not at first sight possess any particular characteristics that would permit us to predict their behavior in situations where mass extermination becomes the rule. The ordinary person is thus the person who we wouldn't necessarily imagine becoming a killer, and who in the aftermath would turn out to be just as banal as they were before. The enigma of their participation in mass atrocity, in the end, is all the greater.

This idea is so widely shared that even the bloodiest, most horrific killers—those who commit the most sordid crimes in periods of civil peace, such as serial killers—are today first considered as ordinary individuals so that the brutality animating them can then be interrogated. For the psychiatrist Daniel Zagury, one of the preeminent French specialists studying serial killers, their potential mental pathologies make them no less ordinary people.[5] As such, this qualification has ultimately become a condensed formula for reminding us that these killers are still part of the human species; they are not, unfortunately, beyond it, despite the horror of their deeds. The term "ordinary" here denotes nothing other than a moral category. Its heuristic value is always summed up in the reminder that the inhumanity of killers remains within the realm of human possibility.

If, however, we want to grant this reference to the ordinary any value in the cases of mass killers, we must avoid any ontological category of "the ordinary person." On the contrary, we must instead interrogate the *ordinary life* of mass killers empirically, focusing on those minor subordinates who are the most docile accomplices to the major crimes of contemporary history. In other words, we must understand how their *forms of life* are declined—forms of life within which these men and sometimes women inhabit their quotidian realities and live them each day, while for all others, the only horizon is violent death. By borrowing the concepts of "the ordinary" and of "forms of life" from the Wittgensteinian tradition—and in particular from their appearance in the work of the Indian-American anthropologist Veena Das[6]—this book undertakes a veritable descent into the ordinary lives of minor actors. The notions of forms of life and of the ordinary allow us to describe their social, psychic, and even biological conditions of life, connecting them with the forms they take in language. Forms of life are thus necessarily plural; they are revealed in the practices, affect, thoughts, and communication of those who share the same living space—the words that they use, the grammar of their feelings. If the ordinary is what presents itself beneath our eyes with evidentiary force, it is also what escapes us regularly; it is taken for granted to the point of being ignored.

How are those conditions lived, which *a posteriori* are revealed to have been exceptional, but were not so at the moment they occurred? How do people represent their lived universe to themselves, when the rest of time and the verdict of history remain unknown? To return to the ordinary means to reintroduce the quotidian into our analysis of major events as they appear to those who live them in the moment or in the immediate aftermath—at a time when the things that we condemn today are accepted, if not valorized. In other words, it is to sound the form of life in which men grow used to executing dozens if not hundreds of individuals each day—just as others go to the factory, the office, or the university.

# 1

# THOSE WHO KILL

Between April 1975, the date Khmer Rouge forces first entered Phnom Penh, and January 1979, the date of their expulsion by Vietnamese troops, over one-third of the Cambodian population was killed. Although the troops' arrival in the capital on April 17, 1975, was meant to signal the end of the war, Pol Pot's regime managed to eliminate almost two million people in less than four years. Set in motion by the Khmer Rouge's seizure of power in the absence of any armed resistance, this crime was not part of any war, civil or otherwise. Instead, it was a systematic purification organized and carried out by the authorities of the time.[1] Forty years later, the main responsible parties were finally brought to justice, despite the absence of their leader, Pol Pot (alias Brother Number One), who had died in the jungle in 1998. Kaing Guek Eav ("Duch") was sentenced to life in the court of appeals in February 2012; he had been the head of the

S-21 prison camp in Phnom Penh where more than 15,000 people were tortured before being killed and thrown into mass graves in Choeung Ek, several miles from the capital. The last two of the regime's high-ranking members still living at the moment of the trial, second-in-command Nuon Chea,[2] and president of Democratic Kampuchea Khieu Samphan, were also sentenced to life in prison in November 2018.[3]

## THE CONFESSIONS

Over the course of the trial, the audience's notes—like the testimonies of civilians, which were included for the first time in proceedings of this scale—provided an unprecedented set of materials relating to the quotidian reality of a genocidal regime. In them, we discover that for the Khmer Rouge at the time, the difference between life and death was simply a bureaucratic decision. During his trial, Duch confessed to almost the totality of the crimes of which he was accused. Certainly, the proof was damning: The S-21 archives, the photographs of the tortured, and thousands of pages of confessions extracted under torture and annotated in his handwriting made it impossible for his defense to plead innocence. A guilty plea was also the condition set by his French co-lawyer, François Roux. A renowned defense lawyer and specialist in civil disobedience and conscientious objection, Roux had agreed to defend the indefensible in the name of his guiding values: the denunciation of the misdeeds of blind obedience and the defense of disobedience when the rule, the law, or the order is unjust. The case of Duch gave him the occasion to plead attenuating circumstances and to ask for mercy for a man who fell victim to his passion for order and obedience. Up until the very last moments of his trial, Duch played his role perfectly, cooperating with the tribunal and correcting witnesses' historical mistakes even when it worked against him.[4] Agreeing to be filmed by the Cambodian director Rithy Panh, he was docile before the camera and willingly furnished details that had previously been unknown.[5] Rejecting the accusation of having killed with his own hands, Duch nevertheless took full responsibility for giving orders. A professor of mathematics and lover of French literature, he took pleasure in describing himself as a rigorous and respectful man, just as slavishly obeying the president of the tribunal's requests for clarification as he had the leaders of the Khmer Rouge. From his point of view, there was very little difference between agreeing to respond to a recognized authority's questions, such as the president of the tribunal's, and assassinating those whom Democratic Kampuchea considered enemies and traitors. In both cases, obedience was only the result of the ordering authority's legitimacy.

To general surprise, however, Duch reversed course at the final moment of the trial, requesting his freedom against the counsel of his French co-lawyer, who was abruptly fired ten days before the verdict was announced. This dismissal was the subject of much discussion, including by Roux himself; it was seen as the will of the dominant regime and its desire to be done with the trial. But the accused's argumentative logic deserves closer attention. In fact, Duch did not request acquittal by claiming he had simply been a soldier following orders, like one more Eichmann capitalizing on the servile obedience of an officer toward his superiors. The head of S-21 went much further. He claimed that he regretted the deaths of innocent people and apologized to the families of those who were unjustly executed. But the innocent only—this was the substance of his claim. The others, traitors and enemies of Democratic Kampuchea, had to have been done away with, the conditions and techniques used to achieve this being much less important than their effectiveness. If any crime had indeed occurred, he claimed, it had been a political one. And for Duch, a political crime was not a crime but a politics. He was thus not to be held guilty for a politics developed by others that he had simply applied with the rigor of a good police chief. Besides, he said, if the Khmer Rouge had won, he would be a hero, not a suspect. Had he not dreamed of being awarded the title of "the Party's best instrument"? In Panh's film, from the depths of his prison, this is what he still regrets, disappointed at having come so close.[6] Duch's case is tragically exemplary of the kinds of men who have not hesitated to send hundreds, thousands, and even hundreds of thousands of men, women, and children to their deaths for obscure ideological reasons. In this sense, these men do resemble Eichmann and so many others like him who, despite their differences, all make the odious justification that the administration of death should be considered a form of politics.

But Duch and Eichmann, like many other intermediaries in these genocidal enterprises, reject the very idea of having had a hand in murder. They gave orders but they did not kill with their own hands. Duch said that he could never have stood it; the idea of it disgusted him; he would have felt too bad, physically, he would have become faint or nauseous and would certainly have lost credibility in the eyes of his subordinates.[7] This was an essential point of his argument: The proof of his lack of direct physical participation in mass atrocity ultimately lay in his weak stature and his extreme sensitivity. You need physical strength to torture a man, he claimed, and above all, you can't be too emotional. He, on the other hand, was an intellectual, a cultured, sensitive, and passionate being—in a word, a commander. He gave orders but he did not kill. Of course, to administer death also means to execute by other hands. But it is much rarer that those who kill under orders come before international tribunals. In Cambodia, only a few of these men were summoned, and then simply as witnesses, to strengthen accusations against their commanders. They did not have to respond to their own deeds: About these they said little, if anything at all.

In Indonesia, to use another example, the ordinary executioners who participated in the massacre of more than a million people in 1965 still walk the streets of the capital, represented as the heroes of a flash conflict against political enemies, even if they were unarmed. In the documentary made by Joshua Oppenheimer, they did not hesitate to recreate the macabre gestures of their quotidian killing.[8] These people were also not brought to justice. Outside of these filmed testimonies, very little is known about them or their stories, except for the fact that they don't seem to feel remorse, shame, or guilt. Things unfolded differently in Rwanda. In fact, while those principally responsible for the genocide came before the International Criminal Tribunal for Rwanda in Arusha (Tanzania), the ordinary actors in those massacres fell under the local and collaborative jurisdiction of the Gacaca courts, in which thousands of the accused were heard. The killers' testimonies were widely collected and analyzed, allowing—probably for the first time—for a precise vision of a mass criminal's ordinary life.[9]

This is the knowledge that is most often missing. Sometimes it is missing in the name of reconciliation, sometimes to preserve a well-trained workforce of torturers for other criminal ends (as was the case for certain Latin American dictatorships or in East Germany, where numerous Nazi war criminals quickly found new jobs, as well as in the United States during the Cold War). Most often, however, it is a simple question of numbers: it would be impossible to judge thousands of war criminals, men and women who had never had to answer for or explain their actions. And even if some of them were investigated, having appeared before judges or simply agreed to speak in front of a camera,[10] it seems that there is something about the intimacy of their testimonies that still eludes comprehension. Yet most express themselves openly. They felt nothing particular, no particular horror at their acts. They did not tell themselves that they had no other choice but to commit harm. They only admit to sometimes having felt disgust, to often having experienced fatigue, and to regularly having been tired of repeating the same gestures. These were their only secrets.

## THE KILLERS' TESTIMONIES

The monumental trial of Lieutenant William Calley, who came before U.S. martial court in 1975 for his role in the My Lai massacre, is a striking example of the kinds of testimony given by those behind certain atrocities. The commander of a small infantry division, Lieutenant Calley captured the Vietnamese hamlet of My Lai on March 16, 1968. Although no North Vietnamese communist soldiers were present, more than four hundred people—exclusively women, children, and elderly men—were massacred in the space of a day. American soldiers faced no resistance on the part of the villagers. Despite the involvement of all of his troops, Calley would be the only one summoned and sentenced. During his trial, and in the face of Calley's composure when the names of the civilian victims—again, women, children, and old men—were read, his defense lawyer, Georges Latimer, attempted to solicit some compassion from him, asking whether he had seen that the victims were not soldiers, and what he had thought or felt in the moment. Calley's response, though, remained as clear as it was cold:

> Well, I was ordered to go in there and destroy the enemy. That was my job on that day. That was the mission I was given. I did not sit down and think in terms of men, women, and children. They were all classified the same, and that was the classification that we dealt with, just as enemy soldiers.[11]

Calley responded similarly to the prosecutor, Aubrey Daniel. That day, he insisted, he marked no distinction between a man, a woman, a child, and an old man. He saw no difference between armed combatants likely to fire back and the unarmed civilians his own men had thrown into a ditch before executing by machine gun.[12]

This general context is of course very different from situations in which massacres have been planned, organized, and ordered by the state or its dissidents. From this angle, we should be careful not to assimilate the acts of violence committed during the Vietnam War—despite their number and their nature—with repressive politics that deliberately target civilians, whether to subdue them or to exterminate them. But from the point of view of those directly implicated—the killers, in other words—things are much less dissimilar. Calley's testimony is a dramatic illustration of the killers' stupefying indifference. Even though some of them express remorse after the fact, to listen to them it would seem that a blanket of indifference prevails in the moment itself.

At the peak of protest against the Vietnam War, at the beginning of the 1970s, the Vietnam Veterans Against the War association (VVAW) undertook a major communications effort to denounce the state of veterans returning home from the war and to end the combat.[13] Their main goal was to show that the war had transformed a significant number of American youth into professional killers, afterwards incapable of re-entering society. The demobilization of groups of drafted soldiers at the end of their tours led to thousands of young men, with no other training than what war had provided, sent back into a policed urban environment that was, in their eyes, more hostile than the Vietnamese jungle, where at least they had learned the norms. Haunted men—often alcoholic, often unemployed—were lost in a society in which they struggled to find a place no one wanted to give them. This postwar desperation found frequent expression in American cinema. In Martin Scorsese's *Taxi Driver* (1976), for instance, in which a taxi driver devastated by the war tries to decide whether to commit murders to attain fame or to save lives (using brutal force either way), we find the figure of a man rendered unfit for civilian life by the war. Even more significant is Michael Cimino's 1978 film *The Deer Hunter*, which depicts the quotidian despair of three friends who cannot imagine civilian life, stripped of the proximity to death that obsesses them after the war. Finally, Ted Kotcheff's 1982 *Rambo* also shows an extraordinarily brutal soldier, capable of the bloody, fiery destruction of an entire city in order to regain his honor in a country that refuses to recognize his service.

The commonalities between these different characters correspond fairly exactly to the lived experiences of a vast majority of veterans after their return from Vietnam: namely, an incommensurable gap between what these men—transformed into killing machines—could now offer, and the expectations of a society that was more resistant than ever to the violence they still incarnated. Attention to this dissonance might be seen to have begun in Detroit, from January 31 to February 3, 1971, when at the instigation of the VVAW more than a hundred war veterans, along with a few civilians and military medical personnel, testified publicly about what the war had done to them. Dubbed the "Winter Soldier Investigation," this initiative gave rise to the revelation of the My Lai massacre to the press, but it aimed to go much further.[14] The goal was to show that My Lai was neither an isolated case nor the work of a few bad apples, but the issue of a politics of war that turned each combatant into a potential agent of atrocity. One by one, each participant took the stage to describe in great detail the crimes in which they had personally and directly participated. The self-accusation of soldiers who could have just as easily kept silent was not intended as an act of individual contrition or as a request for pardon. On the contrary, it was clearly stated as a political act whose aim was to denounce the war and to ask for reparations from the American authorities for what the war had done to its participants. In the middle of these testimonies, each more poignant and more shocking than the last, one young man took the stand to attest that at the moment of his acts—he took responsibility for having executed civilians, including children, and raped women before killing them—he did not consider them as crimes. Or more precisely: It was only when he took up his law studies again, and read the Geneva Convention articles concerning war, that he realized that his acts were subject to prosecution as war crimes. But at the time, he said, he did not know, and had felt nothing in particular. These otherwise ordinary men refused to be seen as monsters or as killers. They considered themselves destroyed by the war, rejected by the society that had sent them into hell, and henceforth doomed to the desperate anonymity of unrecognized war crime victims.[15]

Paradoxically, the American psychiatrist Robert Jay Lifton would become these veterans' best advocate. A fierce opponent of nuclear arms, the horror of which he had experienced directly through the lasting damages he observed during his time as an air force psychiatrist in Japan (1951–53),[16] afterwards he would become known for his sustained fight against the war in Vietnam.[17] A psychiatric expert during the My Lai trial, he embraced the causes of the war killers in order to overwhelm the authorities and to shift the burden to the U.S. government.

In his popular book *Home From the War*, Lifton tells the story of the soldiers left to themselves in the inhospitable jungle, surrounded by invisible and pitiless enemies. He investigates the nature of the massacres in which these men were involved, attempting to understand how and why these soldiers ended up as they did. At no moment does Lifton seek to minimize the facts, knowing them too well to do so. Additionally, he was one of the first to elaborate the notion of war neurosis in civilian populations, doing so in order to combat the stigmatization that had characterized such conditions until that point. Later, when Lifton took up his defense of Vietnam veterans involved in war crimes, it was not to normalize war. On the contrary, he wanted above all to reveal its horror, showing that war not only kills victims but also destroys survivors with equal brutality. Those who had formerly been seen as heroes were thus men who had seen horror and who had—in the case of some of them— taken part in it. Lifton was not looking to excuse them; he showed that all of them knew what they were doing. These soldiers, he said, with Lieutenant Calley in charge, indeed committed horrific crimes, but war itself was responsible—especially this war. If other My Lai massacres were not to occur, he argued, and if American youth was not to be transformed into a generation of "baby killers,"[18] the war had to end.

The essence of his argument rested on an analysis of the precise situations in which these war crimes were committed. Emphasizing the extreme level of tension among the soldiers, who were often young men highly trained on a military level but psychologically underprepared, Lifton advanced the idea that in this immediate context, the violence on both sides was such that the usual moral categories were overturned in favor of the preservation of the group to which one belonged. Atrocity thus became the response that these young men were perceived to be the most "appropriate" in an uncommon situation, one in which the enemy's death was a vital necessity, even if as revenge. By introducing the concept of "atrocity-producing situations," Lifton intended to provide proof that the killers manifested a "normal response"—in other words, not a pathological response from an expert point of view, even if it was morally reprehensible.[19] These men still had not lost a sense of their values. Instead, the exact opposite was true: They reserved these values exclusively for their brothers in arms. As for others, the enemies, anything went: assassination, torture, rape, the mutilation of corpses, and so on. Was it that they didn't realize what they were doing in these situations in which violence produced atrocity? Absolutely not, Lifton responded. They knew what they did, and they knew that these things were not to be done—at least not to their neighbors, their brothers, and the members of their group. But it was precisely because they were perfectly conscious of what not to do to their peers that they were convinced of the total legitimacy of doing it to their enemies. In the whole of his defense, Calley would say nothing contrary to this—nor would Duch, nor the Croatian Miroslav Bralo, despite the regrets he expressed before the International Criminal Tribunal for the former Yugoslavia, during which his guilty plea concluded: "I tried to be proud of my actions and to think they were the actions of a successful soldier [. . .] It has taken me years to understand and acknowledge my full responsibility for each of my own actions."[20]

Had these men become monsters? Lifton would not say so. But he never hesitated to pose the potential for them to become so as a threat in his entreaties that the United States come to its senses and stop the war to save a generation facing a fate worse than death: its irreversible transformation into killing machines.

My question here is not whether or not these men were responsible for their acts, or whether war, totalitarianism, or even genocidal utopias might excuse them or, on the other hand, make things worse by providing the possibility for them to commit acts that would otherwise be unacceptable. The aim of this book is not to indict those who commit atrocities, nor is it to enumerate a list of attenuating circumstances. The reader will form their own opinions of these men and their responsibility; I imagine that it would be pointless to try to steer them one way or another. My intention lies elsewhere. It seems to me essential, today, to understand and analyze how these men and women live a quotidian that is suffused with the deaths of others. To my mind, the secret of their lives is not located solely in the enigma of their acts or in the personal motivations that allow them to kill such great numbers. I do not deny that these motivations exist, but they remain singular—unique to each individual, and not transferable from one killer to the next. To attempt a general anthropology of these men and women who agree to lend their support to the most destructive regimes in recent history means paying closer attention to their lives during the years of the massacres: to their emotions, their fears and dislikes, and to their simple quotidian realities. To analyze how these men and women lived during these years—and not only the acts for which they are condemned today—allows us to understand why they committed such crimes, as well as why they did not refuse to commit them. We should not forget that they are the essential cogs in the wheels of death. Without the participation of each one, the killings would not have taken place.

Among the rare worries that most killers manifest—in the facts they present, as well as in the propaganda they make use of—the fear to be seen as a monster takes precedence.[21] Their lawyers are careful on this point, which is always an essential aspect of their arguments. Whether in the case of François Roux in Duch's trial, the defense lawyers for war criminals in the former Yugoslavia, or experts such as Robert Jay Lifton during the hearings for the perpetrators of the My Lai massacre, all use their rhetorical skills to convince the court to judge these men for what they did, of course, but to keep in mind that they were not monsters at the moment of the events, and that they had not become so afterwards.[22] This insistence is somewhat surprising and should be resituated in the context of violence's aftermath in which the former torturers explain themselves. At a distance, without the protection of their ranks or the whole of their social body, and before the evident disapproval of their interlocutors, it would be surprising if the men on trial would not try to minimize their participation in the crimes and did not try to seem simply ordinary human beings.

But this is not the only reason. Indeed, even for those men who did not commit the most extreme horrors, the figure of the monster functions as the ultimate deterrent, the thing with which they are most loathe to be associated. In the history of our conceptions of mass killers, the monster has occupied the figure of absolute evil since antiquity—so absolute, we could say, that it risks losing its political character, which is not the least of its paradoxes.

# 2

## MONSTERS

*Cruelty and* Jouissance

The figure of the monster has long played a key role in the representation of mass murderers. Unlike even the most brutal participants in conventional wars,[1] these men are most often described as bloodthirsty, as capable of killing even defenseless people such as women, children, and the elderly. They are seen to be literally inhabited by an extreme violence that serves their twisted desires to cause extreme pain without risking combat themselves. Painting and literature are both rife with figures of the monster as perverse and stripped of all humanity.[2] Liberated from all moral fetters, the actions of such creatures are dictated by no logic other than that of total *jouissance*: a monstrously sadistic *jouissance* that encompasses even the most extreme violent acts in order to attain the orgasmic climax of killing itself.

Killing as *jouissance*: This is perhaps the case for the most perverse combatants—the monsters—who abandon all forms of humanity for the ends of pleasure alone. Before even the development of psychoanalytic theories of transgressive *jouissance*—the existence of man's so-called sadistic drives, as well as the death drive—the figure of the monster already represented the idea that murder might be explained by the pleasure it provoked in already transgressive individuals.[3] This view, in turn, is a small step away from imagining that mass killers are indeed criminal monsters who seek perverse pleasures, not only allowed but encouraged to assuage their desires by tortuous states, murderous armies, and bloodthirsty militias— as if attaining the right to mass transgression of the law against murder would liberate the whole force of *jouissance*, devastating and unstoppable.

This monster figure that haunts the body of writing on extreme violence in fact encompasses two versions that are very different, almost opposite. In the first, classic model, the monster is the figure *par excellence* of a troubling alterity. Half human and half something else, undefined but always bestial, brutal, violent, cruel, and sadistic, this monster shares some of the human's morphological traits but is, in fact, the opposite of human. This monster does not belong to the human species. It sometimes comes from it (its hideous distortion, for example), but it remains outside. It is resolutely other. The anxiety it generates stems directly from its exteriority to the human species: Because of its alterity, absolutely nothing in human order could stand against it. Its *jouissance* in doing harm is total and without restraint, without any limit besides its own eventual and temporary satisfaction. Its violence is thus unparalleled, sparked by a cruelty that it alone can master. Although singularly terrifying, this monster is fortunately ultimately rare enough to let men sleep at night.

In the second version, by contrast, the monster remains a human potentiality. It can be revealed or awakened by uncommon events. The appetite for violence and the cruelty of this monstrous tendency within the human being are seen to come from a predisposition that is only summarily subdued by the civilizing process. This monster sleeps in each of us, meaning that any "ordinary" person might one day be transformed into an infernal creature capable of the most dire deeds. But unlike the first version of the monster, this awakened monster does not become a distinct other creature. It remains human and is thus all the more terrifying. These two variants regularly coexist at the heart of views that would make mass killers into monsters. The first version, the a-human monster, has often been the material for literature, theatre, and cinema. The second, however, with the paradoxical aid of psychoanalysis, has come to make us believe that, depending on circumstances, every "ordinary man" could potentially become a killer.[4]

More even than scientific findings, it is theatrical and cinematic representations that have contributed the most to establishing the idea of a certain psychic interiority common to anonymous mass killers. Through such representations, especially as they seek to depict the interiority of those who would kill or have already done so, we sometimes come to believe we can imagine their consciousnesses or even ask ourselves what we would have done in their places.[5] Through the devices of fiction, both theater and film provide the occasion to witness the transformation of an ordinary human into a killer. Yet the most frequent and most frightening figure for this, the figure we encounter most often in classical theater and in contemporary cinema, is in fact not the most true to life. It seems to me that the idea of the mass killer as a man doing more or less painful interior battle before giving in to his basest instincts in a failure of conscience—as dramatically useful as this is—is dangerously misleading. It is, however, this tortured, torturing figure that has been installed in the contemporary imagination, making a fundamental perversity into the essence of the bloodthirsty perpetrator.

Released in 1969, Luchino Visconti's famous film *The Damned* is perhaps one of the best examples of this type of portrayal. Made at the high point of Western introspection into the barbarism at the heart of civilization, the film offers a terrifying depiction of the rise of

Nazism through the story of a German haute bourgeois family's fall. The main thrust of the film is the articulation of the Nazi rise to power and the progressive liberation of the most deviant human instincts across all protagonists, culminating in the corruption of every member of the family. For the 2016 Festival d'Avignon, the Belgian director Ivo van Hove adapted Visconti's screenplay for the stage into an even more unsettling iteration, doubling the critique of Nazism with a condemnation of all forms of contemporary inhumanity. The play's resonance with the events of the years 2015 and 2016, punctuated as they were by deadly attacks and major political anxieties,[6] was immediately apparent. It showed the rise of extremism on all sides, as a glorification of hatred for alterity took on alarming strength in so-called democratic countries. For spectators, it seemed, perversion's poison could be bodily felt, slowly infiltrating until the final climax when the audience itself came into the sights of the killer.

The press responded in force. The play was unanimously praised: It was called "a shock" in *Télérama*; "a monster piece," "haunting and unsettling," in *Le Figaro*; a revelation of "the horrific human aptitude for savagery" in *Le Monde*. All critics, including those previously known for their habitual disapproval for the theatrical staging of brutality, were in agreement on the director's work and the performance of the Comédie Française's actors, even as many of them shared a sense of unease about the voyeurism the production entailed for its audiences.

But across the board, van Hove was praised for having been able to bring a terrifying plunge into inhumanity to life before an astounded audience. Spectators were spared nothing: perversion, incest, decadence, disgrace, greed, baseness, and even the most bloodthirsty (and bloodiest) murder. Onstage, bodies reveled in lust and in blood with the same degree of morbid excitement. It seemed that nothing could stop the infernal descent and that death, although inevitable, was not the nadir—the worst was present as early as the very first transgression.

In van Hove's adaptation, as in Visconti's film, the tipping point is reached very early in the course of events. Whether the death of the patriarch or barely repressed incestuous desire, the staging of some first inaugural mistake or transgression prefigures the infernal rest in which all—truly all—horrors become possible, because now all is permitted. The equation set forth is both simple and chilling. The first transgression liberates the most violent, sickest tendencies and clears the way for a limitless *jouissance* that makes the other into both the instrument and the object of a chilling and devastating hatred. This hatred turns the perversity of *jouissance* into the motor for an abomination that is all the more terrifying because it is authorized. Who—we hear each protagonist ask—would possibly give up such pleasure if there is no sanction against it and no consequences for it?

If this *mise en abyme* of the worst human passions so astonishes us, however, and if the horror becomes terrifyingly palpable, this is above all because both the filmmaker and the director seek in their own ways to offer the audience a representation of unrepresentable genocidal destruction. Both transpose the accession of a totalitarian and genocidal regime into the double register of the decline of civilization on the one hand, and the vilest human passions on the other. If this transposition is so effectively striking, it nevertheless remains fundamentally outside the reality and the organization of mass crimes.

For real-life killers, first and foremost, things are often much simpler. The reign of perversity is simply not always necessary. The moral dilemmas, hesitations of conscience, and pangs of doubt that accompany fictional or dramatic characters all the way up until the climax, when they finally abandon themselves to their desires and feast upon the suffering of the other, are rarely present in the quotidian life of perpetrators. And above all, such qualms are useless—even damaging—to the proper functioning of extermination processes. The genocidal universe is precisely not a world where everything is possible. It is quite the opposite. These worlds are marked by order and by method, by a quest for productivity, and by the evolution of working conditions that let killers continue to kill at an accelerating rate. The whole of the process happens according to a sequencing that has been perfectly calibrated, from the selection of victims to their grouping, from their execution to the methodical management of remains (the corpses, the objects that have been taken from them). Nothing is left to chance. Nothing remains arbitrary, and certainly nothing is left to any sadistic drives that would eventually slow productivity and become blunted as an effect of repetition. Only order prevails. Every genocidal society operates in this way, compartmentalizing populations and designating those who must die and those who will be spared.[7] Each compartment has its own rules: Here again, all is not permitted. For those destined for death, selection is merciless but what happens at the beginning matters little, and what alone counts is the final destruction. In the other compartment, killing is forbidden and subject to heavy punishment. Only the transfer from one side to the other due to betrayal, for example, would authorize the killing of an individual who was previously on the side of the spared. The stories of ordinary torturers and executioners all attest to this reality: To kill in great number requires a complex organization that would never be possible to subject to each individual's intimate passions.

How, then, do we account for the popularity of the monster and its abominations in the contemporary imaginary? An answer lies in the function that the monster has held beyond the question of killers alone. In other words, the construction should be resituated in the bigger whole of ideas surrounding the civilization process. Here, Norbert Elias's thought is particularly instructive. In the first volume of his 1939 work *The Civilizing Process*, published in English as *The History of Manners*,[8] Elias puts forth the idea that the progressive acquisition of civilized principles is accompanied by an individual interiorization of the taboo and the limits of the possible, thanks to mechanisms of self-restraint that censure improper, indecent, or violent behaviors. This censure means that killing for extermination, for example, becomes not simply a social interdiction but a subjective impossibility, accompanied by a revulsion as powerful as the "horror of incest." In Elias's view, such transgressions are inconceivable on the scale of an entire population whose accession to the highest level of the civilizing process is necessarily accompanied by a radical and definitive repression of the most violent instincts. Of course certain individuals are capable of them, but their transgression represents an isolated breach of social limits, otherwise insurmountable, and above all the effacement of the subjective borders that mark out the human in each individual. The monster is here seen as the figure of an isolated failure, an ephemeral moment in the process of civilization. Its existence can thus be considered proof of the success of the majority of the others, and of the most effective and most irreversible self-control that pushes everyone—even mass killers themselves—to hold this abominable figure in the utmost contempt. Thus the monster's cautionary role stems less from its accord with the reality of killing practices than from the idea it incarnates of a fall into a darker world. In representing or incarnating an absolute evil, the construction of the monster paradoxically turns the "civilizing process" into humanity's best guarantee against the return of barbarism.[9]

But with the revelation of the concentration camps, the Second World War would resound as the most categorical refutation of the civilizing illusion. This was not a case of one or two men having been transformed into monsters, nor even dozens or hundreds, but thousands or even entire populations supporting or acting in service of the most extreme cruelty. The monster figure outlined above as both the incarnation of absolute evil and an exceptional failure or aberration of the civilizing process could in no way account for the sophistication and the industrialization of executions and the emotional coldness with which the extermination of several million human beings had been planned and methodically carried out by the Nazis.

For Elias, the history of the mid-twentieth century meant a total repudiation of his previous work. He undertook this via the idea of a hypothetical process of "decivilization" to explain this upsurge of violence and cruelty that so brutally ruined the civilizational work that the German people had exemplified in his eyes.[10] He had to admit that this society had undergone a very fast process of annihilating the gains of civilization; the great majority of its individuals had returned to a stage that pre-existed social evolution, an era at which self-control was not yet powerfully established. As this occurred, the extrinsic radicality of the monster shaded into a more ambiguous and more worrying figure—a sort of human avatar in which each person might be able to recognize themselves.

In the title of his provocative 2013 essay—*Aurais-je été bourreau ou résistant*, or roughly "would I have been a killer or a member of the resistance," in English—Pierre Bayard sets out to explore a question that has been posed since World War II and still troubles many of his contemporaries today. To do so, he employs a unique narrative method: a sort of autobiography of a fictional double, who possesses all of the author's psychological attributes—his emotions, his rationales, his feelings and his doubts—but who takes his own father's birth date and childhood during the major events that preceded and accompanied the French defeat and the German occupation. To ask these questions at the heart of a work that mixes personal and familial memories is obviously a brave undertaking. And even the most seasoned researchers into the historical conditions that favored the fall of millions of innocent-seeming individuals into barbarism regularly approach the question of what "they themselves would have done in the same situation."[11] This is Bayard's challenge: He will tell us what he would have done—or at the very least, he concedes, he will try to approach the question as honestly as possible.

Certainly there is no doubting the author's signature brilliance.[12] Here, as in previous works, his writing is daring and sharp. The framework he employs, however, is much more conventional, situated in our particular historical moment at which the Nazi executioner, after having been considered the archetype of absolute evil, is now thought to be culturally closer to us,[13] our troubling *semblable*, making us shudder at the idea of ourselves as potential killers. This perception, as we have just seen, is grounded on a reversal by which those who, following Norbert Elias, formerly believed in the unshakable virtues of civilizing utopias came to be convinced of the opposite: that from now on everything is terribly possible, hidden in each individual's darkest depths. It has thus become possible to imagine that everyone—or rather, anyone—is in the intrinsic possession of all the elements necessary to become a killer if the conditions are unfortunately propitious. Yet the adjective "intrinsic" is the most problematic here; it presupposes a psychic potentiality that, depending on the circumstances, might rise to light, pushing individuals toward the choice of barbarism. This is the direction in which Bayard's work leads us to think. "For a Freudian," he writes, "there is nothing at all enigmatic about the slippage towards the shadows; it is part of the logic of psychic functioning to give free rein to violent drives when society's barriers collapse."[14] It is not surprising that such an affirmation proclaims its affiliation with Sigmund Freud. The majority of those who today still fear that evil lurks in the depths of the individual soul or psyche share a common understanding of Freud's work. They are sometimes the same who—in the name of Freud's legacy—suggest a form of indulgence or even mercy toward executioners, in the name of the principle that they, the killers, are closer to us than we would ever have imagined.[15]

Nevertheless, a return to Freud's writing on war complicates this reading, which is perhaps too alarmist, in favor of an entirely different perspective that is not necessarily more reassuring but is no more worrisome, either. Freud is not attempting to analyze war, nor is he looking into its political and economic motives. Still less is he concerned with certain states' appetites for conquest and domination. Despite a sometimes widespread view to the contrary among his critics as well as his followers, Freud is not playing political apprentice—in other words, he is not attempting to psychoanalyze war, looking in the unconscious for deeper motives that have driven people to conflict since the beginning of time. In this, he distances himself from the hypothesis of a "human nature" that is intrinsically troubling, from which the worst catastrophes can always emerge. Instead, he seeks to understand why the basest elements sometimes triumph during the course of war. Or more precisely, he investigates the unconscious reasons for which certain men take advantage of the particular context of war to commit acts otherwise thought to be impossible. This approach is, in fact, likely to illuminate the ease with which certain men give in to extreme violence, but it does not presuppose that human violence is psychically determined.

Written in the turmoil of the beginning of World War I, and published in 1915, Freud's "Thoughts for the

Times on War and Death"[16] sets out a psychoanalytic perspective on the part of the human psyche that renders the violence of war possible. Like the majority of his contemporaries, Freud very quickly became troubled by the brutality of this war, and wanted to take account of the psychic processes that might be able to explain an upsurge of violence on the part of men who, several years beforehand, had shown no tangible sign of such a possibility. A man of his time, little inclined to contest the legitimacy of this war and partisan to the idea of ultimate sacrifice to defend one's country,[17] Freud would rarely make allowances for those who attempted to shirk their military obligations, whether for ideological or psychiatric reasons (neurosis, particularly).[18] In this, he differed from his pupil Victor Tausk, who courageously defended war deserters by seeking to demonstrate, from a psychoanalytic perspective, that their decision stemmed not from a deliberate choice to commit treason. Instead, for Tausk, it represented a psychic collapse linked to the nature of combat and the loss of comrades that left them no other psychic or concrete alternative than to flee. For Freud, war has its own reasons that do not correspond to the psychic necessity that is the domain of the unconscious. The psychoanalyst Karl Abraham, who would have a strong influence on future psychoanalytic conceptions of war neuroses, held that it was an individual's duty to take up arms to defend their country. Those who wished to avoid this should be considered pathological cases—too selfish and too narcissistic to put their lives at risk to save the nation.[19] In other words, neither Freud nor Abraham saw war as an aberration stemming directly from a primitive violence inherent in the human psyche. Instead, they were clear, wars had political, economic, or territorial reasons on which psychoanalysis ultimately had very little impact. On the other hand, though, the way in which men behaved during war was indeed the domain of psychoanalytic investigation. This is an essential nuance. It is exactly this approach that Freud set forth in his work on war and death, and that he would revisit in a later text, published in 1933 at the moment of the rise of Nazism, soberly titled "Why War?"[20]

The 1915 text is constructed around the hypothesis that war is likely to foster regression to earlier stages of psychic development, back to those stages still governed by the most primitive impulses. In this psychoanalytic perspective, the progressive acquisition of unconscious psychological repressions happens through the intermediary of a process of the layering of impulses, more or less developed or more or less primitive, that will progressively be repressed and eventually give way to the higher layers that are most conducive to the functioning of contemporary man. For all that, though, nothing in the psyche disappears completely, and Freud adds that "the primitive mind is, in the fullest meaning of the word, imperishable."[21] Indeed, the higher forms of development remain the most vulnerable, whereas the primitive instincts remain unchanged in each individual's unconscious even though their expression has been forbidden by psychological development. War, Freud writes, very quickly dissolves these upper layers and thus permits the liberation of primitive instincts in which violence, hate, and primal destructivity win out.

But immediately Freud qualifies this first proposition, emphasizing that what happens at the level of the drives and impulses does not necessarily have a corresponding equivalent in reality. It is possible to do good for bad unconscious reasons, or to do harm for good ones. In other words, Freudian thought indeed helps us understand how certain wartime situations are liable to liberate impulses that are otherwise repressed, but it does not seek to account either for the phenomenon of war in its entirety or for military activity. The latter would be the object of a later study, in 1921, in *Group Psychology and the Analysis of the Ego*.[22] What Freud attempts to explain in this work, though, is in no way comparable to the surging of drives he analyzes in "Thoughts for the Times." It is, in fact, the opposite; for Freud, the army is among those hyper-organized bodies—on the model of obsessional neurosis—where the reigning order aims (as it does in civilian life) to control most potential individual primitive impulses using bodily discipline, obedience, and submission to authority all the way up to military strategy or the laws of war.

It is thus neither the army nor military action but simply certain aspects of war that are not only capable of "un-repressing" motions previously held back in the unconscious but also of satisfying another unconscious tendency that departs from the pleasure principle that Freud had just identified.[23] The introduction of the death drive in 1920 adds an additional element into the Freudian structure. This drive is separate from the archaic remnants and remains present at numerous levels of civil life; it has the ability to reinforce the most extreme predilections of those who, plunged into the violence of war, have already let their most primitive instincts show through. The conjunction of these two processes has the power to transform ordinary men into "monsters" at any moment, capable of terrible atrocities and worst of all likely to enjoy the exercise of absolute power over the lives of others.

Thus, in light of this thinking, the monster dwells potentially in each individual and can be revealed at any moment if, in a sudden turn of history, the social conditions make way for it. Yet despite its darkness, the 1933 text is significantly more ambiguous and tempers this prophesy. Its historical context is, of course, essential. At the time of its publication, Germany had just fallen to the Nazis, and Austria was beginning to be overtaken by the same fervor. As Freud observed the contagion and dissemination of hatred with deep sadness, Albert Einstein suggested he write a short text on the psychological determinants of war and the scientific possibilities for counteracting its effects. Einstein had been tasked by the League of Nations with the project of bringing together the leading scientists of the time in order to inventory contemporary knowledge of war—not only to analyze the conditions of its possibility but ultimately to promote scientific perspectives that could protect contemporary nations against the return of barbarism. In the end, Freud was not particularly receptive to his eminent colleague's arguments, and not especially inclined to engage in deep interdisciplinary dialogue. His only response was a brief crepuscular text whose pessimism makes it still subject to debate today.[24]

Unlike Elias, who thought that the process of civilization insured us against the return of the darkest passions thanks to the interiorization of self-control,[25] Freud did not believe in the existence of such protection, at least not in the unconscious. Do not think—he tells us—that there are subterranean forces that stop men from committing the most extreme acts during wartime. There are not. Or more precisely: Even if they exist, this in no way predicts their occurrence in reality. But do not believe either, he continues, that even more primitive forces, a sort of call to the death drive, will necessarily rise up to compel these men to commit atrocities. These forces exist, and the war offers them a great territory over which to expand, of course—but the psyche knows neither good nor evil. In fact, as he had written in "Thoughts for the Times," "a human being is seldom altogether good or bad."[26] Archaic and violent forces can be converted into altruistic passions that can bring incontestable good— as, for example, in the case of an individual fascinated by bodies and blood who finds a way to satisfy morbid impulses in the practice of surgery while nevertheless saving many lives. On the other hand, the impulses seen to be more altruistic and humanist, fundamentally oriented towards the good of all—like a mother sacrificing herself for the good of her child—can lead some individuals to invent extraordinarily coercive political organizations, in which the elimination of those who resist is seen as a necessary good and a just sacrifice.

In characteristic fashion, Freud rejects deterministic explanations and opposes those who still imagine basing the ability to discern good from evil in the unconscious. He insists otherwise, striving to put our illusions to rest.[27] Psychoanalysis teaches not only that man is ultimately not the master of himself, but also that he is not the best guarantor of the species. He is neither good nor bad, simply because these questions are not based in the psyche. This, in a nutshell, is Freud's response to Einstein. It is understandable that Einstein emerged less than pleased from this brief exchange. While the physicist hoped to find in depth psychology the beginnings of a solution that would elevate man past the point of any return to monstrosity, the psychoanalyst responded that no more was the antidote to the monster hidden in the depths of the human psyche than was the monster itself. The two could coexist, giving rise to ultimately anything. It was thus better not to have too much faith that man would one day find a miraculous cure for rendering himself incapable of atrocity. This is the disillusion that Freud asked his contemporaries to consider during the troubled period when the worst case appeared again inevitable. He had already formulated this caution in response to those who, toward the end of World War I, expressed their terrible disappointment in humanity. For the father of psychoanalysis, their disappointment should not have been so great—for "in reality," as he wrote, "our fellow-citizens have not sunk so low as we feared, because they had never risen so high as we believed."[28]

Taken together, "Thoughts for the Times" and "Why War?" do not address questions of mass killings. At the time they were published, the horror remained limited to the misconduct, albeit horrible and frequent, that accompanied battles. The most horrible violence had not yet come, or rather was not yet recognized[29]—it was not even imaginable despite what would become the planning and execution of a vast plan of the extermination of civilian populations. These two texts, however, do help explain what happened several years later among killers who would act with an almost unparalleled cruelty in the grip of sadistic and primitive impulses—such as the Ustaše Petar Brzica, who, before disappearing into exile, bragged about having killed 1,360 Serb and Jewish prisoners over the course of World War II in the infamous Jasenovac concentration camp, armed only with a knife called a *srbosjek*, or literally, "Serb killer." Specifically designed for repeated, quick, and effortless killings of hundreds of prisoners, the weapon was made up of a leather glove into which was set a 12-centimeter blade molded to the curve of a prisoner's neck. These types of assassins, unfortunately, are found by the hundreds, or even thousands, in all contexts of mass atrocity, mass extermination, ethnic purification, and of course genocide. It is men of such brutality who have crystallized the attention of contemporary thinkers seeking to penetrate the mystery of violence, investigating the psychological way this potential might have been liberated thanks to the collapse of collective and individual repression of deathly impulses.

The faces of these men, still, are often known to us. Their names still make us tremble; their memories raise in us all sorts of complex memories, mixing terror, incomprehension, disgust, and desire for vengeance; we even, sometimes, hope to make them undergo what they did to others in the flesh. Whether they were already bloodthirsty killers—monsters, in other words—or whether war and mass violence transformed them and awakened their most primitive drives ultimately changes nothing. They have long occupied our imaginary, making us believe that their individual fall into the darkest depths explains their collective cruelty. It might begin to seem as if the only explanation of the massacres of yesterday and today is that these men have all become monsters, prey to their most primitive instincts and ruled by the death drive alone. Yet the problem lies precisely in this false inference. However many of the most bloodthirsty killers fit into this psychoanalytic explanation, the results of all their criminal actions could never add up to the stupefying number of victims across the various processes of mass extermination that have occurred since the mid-twentieth century. It is precisely because other men—much more numerous than these first—also participate in massacres that extermination processes are able to happen as horrifically as they do.

Freudian theory did not anticipate that these "monster-men" would represent only an infinitesimal minority of those who participated and would participate in the mass atrocities of our age. Indeed, most actors are ordinary individuals who have no need even to mobilize their sadistic impulses or death drives to commit massacres of defenseless civilians or killings of families, villages, and entire populations, and to commit these acts as part of their regular lives, not in the mental state of mass murderers. Here lies the true enigma that psychoanalysis cannot resolve. None of its principal hypotheses—neither the return of the primitive, sadistic impulses nor the death drive—allow for an understanding of how these men carry out such crimes in the most ordinary way. This is the question that both Hannah Arendt's notion of the "banality of evil" and Christopher Browning's idea of "ordinary men" attempt to address.

# 3

# ORDINARY MAN
# AND HIS PATHOLOGIES

In my report of [the Eichmann trial in Jerusalem] I
spoke of "the banality of evil." Behind that phrase, I
held no thesis or doctrine, although I was dimly aware
of the fact that it went counter to our tradition of
thought—literary, theological, or philosophic—about
the phenomenon of evil. Evil, we have learned, is
something demonic; its incarnation is Satan [. . . or
those who] don't want to serve God but to be like
Him. Evil men, we are told, act out of envy [. . .] Or
they may be prompted by weakness [. . .] Or, on the
contrary, by the powerful hatred wickedness feels for
sheer goodness [. . .]. However, what I was confronted
with was utterly different and still undeniably factual.
I was struck by a manifest shallowness in the doer that
made it impossible to trace the uncontestable evil of
his deeds to any deeper level of roots or motives. The

deeds were monstrous, but the doer—at least the very effective one now on trial—was quite ordinary, commonplace, and neither demonic nor monstrous. There was no sign in him of firm ideological convictions or of specific evil motives, and the only notable characteristic one could detect in his past behavior as well as his behavior during the trial and throughout the pre-trial police examination was something entirely negative: it was not stupidity but *thoughtlessness*.[1]

Hannah Arendt introduced her spring 1972 Gifford Lecture, "The Life of the Mind," delivered at the University of Aberdeen, with these lines. For her, a return to her notion of the banality of evil provided an occasion to respond to the critiques—sometimes severe— that had been leveled against her 1963 report, *Eichmann in Jerusalem*.[2] This polemic had been attacked by philosophers from all corners; criticism came from Arendt's habitual detractors, of course, but also from some of her closest friends. In her capacity as a reporter for the *New Yorker*, Arendt had attended the trial of the Nazi officer Adolf Eichmann, which was held in Jerusalem starting in April of 1961. Responsible for putting the final solution into motion during the Third Reich, Eichmann was able to flee when the Nazis surrendered. Discovered by the Israeli secret service in Argentina, he was captured and secretly deported to Israel for the trial. Unlike the Nuremberg Trials, which were held several years earlier and aimed at the entirety of Nazi crimes, Eichmann's trial was seen as the trial for the final solution and consequently for the extermination of several million Jews. In light of the event's monstrosity, the Israeli court wanted in turn to show the monstrosity of the men who had imagined, planned, and carried out this unprecedented crime. Eichmann became simultaneously its symbol and its principal actor; the verdict, like his sentence, was to provide an occasion for the denunciation of the totality of the crime and to make its sponsors into the product of an aberration whose exceptionality—in all senses of the term—must be forever inscribed into collective memory.

But far from embracing this line of reasoning, Arendt would deliver a much less consensual "report." Uncompromising, she attacked the trial's procedures, the partisan interests of its Israeli directors, and above all the leadership of the Jewish Councils (*Judenrat*) that she accused of being involved with the Nazi authorities, especially as they underestimated the risks and thus facilitated the deportation of members of their own communities. Although they were condemned by the intellectual figures who provided the foundations for Arendt's own analyses of Jewish extermination in Europe, such as Raul Hilberg,[3] these caustic attacks deserve to be recontextualized in the general project of Arendt's thesis. Over the course of the dispatches she delivered to the *New Yorker*, she endeavored to draw attention away from the figure of Eichmann alone, above all to lessen the impact of a false personification of the event.

If Arendt's work in *Eichmann in Jerusalem* hinges primarily on deconstructing such personification, this is essentially in the service of her thinking on totalitarianism, published a decade earlier.[4] The political history of totalitarianism that she seeks to establish rests first on showing the different components of the quest for power. This quest occurs neither through the individual militancy of the most fervent or engaged leaders nor through the more or less active participation of their political supporters. Many other factors, taken together, make totalitarian regimes possible. Key here is the guilty negligence of other actors in the face of rising totalitarian fantasies. This includes both the passivity of the masses and the unfounded optimism of the elite, who think they can live with the whims of their unsophisticated leaders and hope to manipulate them for their own profit. In the case of Nazism, these different factors quickly converged, facilitating the seizure of power by Hitler and his troops and end of democracy in March of 1933.[5]

Arendt applies this same paradigm to her coverage of Eichmann's trial. For her, Eichmann was not "the" responsible party, although she maintained that he was guilty of what he had done, both in terms of his acts and his orders. But where the court sought the most damning evidence against him as the main author of the crime,

Arendt followed the clues that would demonstrate how Eichmann alone could never have done what he did without the participation of thousands of others, and not only those who were his subordinates. In support of her thesis, Arendt would deploy two very different types of arguments. Together they would produce the desired effect, which was the opposite of the trial taking place before her eyes. The first argument rests on an examination of the nature of the criminal organization and its ramifications, which were widespread at the most *a priori* unsuspected levels. It is because totalitarian regimes benefit from the complicity of different types of groups—via the terror they impose, the extortion they exercise, or the use of any other technique that aims to manipulate different social bodies—that they are able to keep an entire society in check, to eliminate all those who resist or whom they have decided to exterminate. Arendt's insistence on denouncing the complicity of Jewish Councils deserves to be revisited in this perspective. In effect, in showing that Jewish institutions agreed to deal with the Nazi regime to spare certain lives, it seems to me that Arendt sought less to condemn these institutions (as she was endlessly accused of having done at the time) than to emphasize that Eichmann ultimately benefitted from countless complicities, including those of some of his "victims." By insisting on this point, Arendt is not blaming the victims, as she is still today wrongly accused of having done. Rather, she reveals the deep workings of totalitarianism: specifically, its terrible ability to infiltrate all levels of society and to lead individuals—even those who would naturally be the most opposed—to act according to its directions alone, without even any need to "convert" them to its reasoning or its ideology. In this way, the instances of Jewish collaboration were nothing other than a concrete demonstration of this principle. In the same way, her charge against the Israeli officials, who wanted to turn the trial into a historically momentous condemnation of the principle behind the Jewish massacre, deserves to be understood as the denunciation of any attempt to personify the crime, which would be to the detriment of an incontrovertible indictment of totalitarianism.

This first line of attack thus did not seek to exculpate Eichmann. Even less did it attempt to diminish his responsibility in the whole of the totalitarian process—far from it. The second argument would let Arendt definitively bring down the accused, attacking his character directly—not only for what he did, but also for what he was. Everything in the previous history of this man had suggested mediocrity, pettiness, and the cowardly ambition that would find an unexpected outlet in his affiliation with Nazism. By adhering to Hitler's party, as she wrote, "Somebody like him—already a failure in the eyes of his social class, of his family, and hence in his own eyes as well—could start from scratch and still make a career."[6] Bit by bit, she deconstructs the figure of the fervent ideologue and the remorseless decision-maker, as he was made out to be, to reveal the personality of a "thoughtless" man who had really neither the intellectual capacity nor the personal authority of the high-ranking political official that the trial was seeking to substantiate. This thinking was also the logic behind her argument with the Israeli government, which in her view wanted to use Eichmann to construct the image of a demonic power that the Jewish state could punish, rather than to take account of the real personality of the accused. Of course he was an essential cog in the wheels of death, but not the most important one, and certainly not for the person he was. Not only did he benefit from the participation and the complicity of thousands of people, but as a man, he himself would have been incapable of imagining, executing, and carrying this crime on his shoulders alone. By showing Eichmann as mediocre, little, petty, ridiculous, and even pitiful—in a word, banal—Arendt wanted to demonstrate that history had made him into something he absolutely was not: an important man.

Arendt introduces the notion of the "banality of evil" in order to account for this contradiction between the monstrous history of totalitarianism and the mediocrity of the men who served it. Neither a key concept nor the framework for a doctrine of totalitarianism, the banality of evil comes down to a simple empirical claim that neither explains nor excuses totalitarianism but is simply regularly associated with it. For Arendt, the banality of evil is thus synonymous not only with mediocrity, accumulated minor cowardice, lack of empathy or judgment, and of course lack of intelligence, but above all lack of thought. She describes Eichmann as an ordinary man and nothing more—in other words, a man who was in no way exceptional on an intellectual level, in terms of personal history, or even in the nature of his convictions. He was "ordinary, commonplace, and neither demonic nor monstrous,"[7] and for exactly these reasons he had to be brought to justice for his acts. This, I think, is the first lesson that should be drawn from Arendt's famous phrase. It is because Eichmann was an ordinary man that he was subject to human justice. Removing all ontological monstrosity, Arendt renders Eichmann answerable to the law and fundamentally responsible for his acts—unlike the monsters and other abnormal beings that had seemed to be outside of justice from the beginning of the nineteenth century onwards.[8]

The second essential lesson has to do with the correlation Arendt establishes between ordinary men and mediocrity. By highlighting the degree to which Eichmann was simply an ordinary human being, Arendt does not make him into an "everyman." On the contrary, she characterizes him according to his mediocrity: mediocrity of character, of personal and affective history, of ambition, and even of career. And yet neither mediocrity nor banality explains the crime; they are simply only favorable conditions. The origin of the crime is in totalitarianism, to which men submit with more or less ease, complacency, or stupidity, but always with full awareness, whether they enjoy it or not. These men also know how to profit from what crime alone will allow, and this makes them even more responsible for their acts—in short, guilty.

It is not my intention here to give a detailed commentary on Hannah Arendt's oeuvre; this has already been largely accomplished by philosophers, historians, and political scientists, as well as sociologists and anthropologists, to such an extent that listing and comparing all the views would be impossible. I want simply to limit my work to remarks on three points: evil, the ordinary, and the executioners whose stories underlie my investigations into the quotidian reality of mass killers.

*Evil*

In fact, Arendt remains dependent on a philosophical and moral understanding of the notion of evil that is ultimately incompatible with the rest of her work. Even as she seeks to demonstrate how this category of analysis does not pertain to the logic behind the functioning of genocide, she nevertheless subtly associates the idea of "evil" with banality, re-introducing a degree of ambiguity. Of course, the acts of genocidaires,[9] and in particular Eichmann's deeds, indisputably represent the climax of evil in its most absolute form. Arendt and all the commentators of the age agreed on this without hesitation. But the force of her demonstration lies in her claim that the idea of evil would not explain the nature and scale of such a crime.

She sets out to do the opposite: to try to penetrate a criminal's thought and to understand how they explained to themselves what they had to do and why they had to do it, remaining as close as possible to their way of seeing things. And this is what gives her perspective, still today, a fundamentally groundbreaking heuristic power, one that would only be developed much later in certain anthropological approaches to genocidal organizations.

And yet when it came to choosing her report's subtitle, she distanced herself from this mental closeness, as if she wanted to collect her wits and move away from the unspeakable, unrestrained horror she had found. To do this, she reintroduces the idea of evil. In so doing, she risks contradicting herself, gesturing toward a sort of exteriority to Eichmann's remarks, which she had meticulously deciphered. Like every other genocidaire who had appeared before the international tribunals after World War II, Eichmann had not lost his sense of good and evil. Instead, like these others, he had simply adjusted the focus, drawing the line between the world of good and the world of evil so radically differently that he, like the majority of these killers, was able to affirm that there was nothing deliberately evil in what had happened. Starting from the beginning of the hearings, moreover, Eichmann's lawyer, Robert Servatius, adopted a line of defense that involved declaring his client had done nothing wrong, that he was being accused not of crimes but of "'acts of state' over which no other state has jurisdiction," and that "he had committed acts 'for which you are decorated if you win and go to the gallows if you lose.'"[10] According to Arendt, for Eichmann himself "the indictment implied not only that he had acted on purpose, which he did not deny, but out of base motives and in full knowledge of the criminal nature of his deeds. As for the base motives, he was perfectly sure that he was not what he called an *innerer Schweinehund*, a dirty bastard in the depths of his heart; and as for his conscience, he remembered perfectly well that he would have had a bad conscience only if he had not done what he had been ordered to—to ship millions of men, women, and children to their death with great zeal and the most meticulous care."[11] This is what distinguishes these mass criminals from common-law ones. While the latter often recognize that they have done "evil" or "harm," the former systematically retreat behind the idea of a collective good that requires sacrifices, sometimes major—sacrifices that they have had the honor of undertaking for what they believe to be a just cause. This is also what Duch, head of the S-21, would say before the Extraordinary Chambers, adding that he was always devoted to doing his job rigorously and with no other passion than the order he served. Even in their guilty pleas, at least some of the torturers who operated in the former Yugoslavia admitted that their acts were abominable only to then recall that in the moment of their happening they thought, on the contrary, that they were serving a just cause.

In other words, revisiting the notion of the banality of evil suggests that it might not be so heuristic after all.

Obviously, banality is evil's principal characteristic—at least when it designates mediocrity—but "evil" as a moral category is decidedly not situated where we might expect to find it. For these killers, evil is uncontestable: It lies in the idea of disobeying orders, failing to accomplish the tasks with which they have been charged, or—worse—proving to be unworthy of their hierarchical superiors' confidence. For men such as Eichmann or Duch, and for many others, this fear of doing "evil" becomes a true obsession. It is the source of their fears and the thing that guides their consciences, acts, and even eventually their regrets and remorse. But it never involves the fate of those who fall victim to their methodical sense of duty.

*The Ordinary*

Was Eichmann really, as Arendt depicted him, a banal and minor functionary, lacking thought and even affirmed ideology, caught up in the nets of bureaucracy? Or should we follow Bettina Stangneth in her deconstruction of Arendtian mythology and her rereading of the history of a truly genocidal man, cold and determined, but able to seem otherwise over the course of his trial?[12] These two versions differ on many points, and their oppositions are determinant for contemporary historiography. But they agree on at least one point. By inflating Eichmann's weakness of character, Arendt seeks above all to minimize his political importance and to better reveal his mediocrity. He was neither monster nor hero, she tells us, but simply a banal and ordinary man. In portraying him as a much more arrogant figure, ambitious and stripped of all care except for himself, Stangneth does not make him less mediocre. Instead, she simply confirms that his mediocrity and banality coexisted with the feeling of superiority conferred on him by the power he held within the Nazi regime. In the end, what we can draw from both readings of Eichmann's personality is that this man was in no way exceptional, and that the events he took part alone in gave him an importance he could otherwise never have assumed.

Rereading Arendt today, it seems to me that what she wanted to accomplish with her version of Eichmann's case was not to define a natural human condition but simply to explain the scorn—not fear—inspired by those who assassinated millions of human beings in a cowardly way. Yet this conception of the ordinary is incompatible with the idea that has since been established by which anyone could become a killer under the right circumstances. This framework, which turns the ordinary into a condition that is ontologically sufficient to explain the possibility of "normal" individuals being transformed into pitiless, remorseless executioners, rests on a naïve and empirically unfounded inversion of Arendt's position. In other words, just because a significant number of so-called ordinary people are found among the men who order or take part in mass killings does not mean that the fact of being ordinary in itself means a greater risk of becoming a killer. This is an absurd syllogism. The more obvious conclusion should be, instead, that the fact of being either a monster or an ordinary man has no predictive value. Either or both of them could turn into a killer—or not.

## The Executioners

As soon, though, as we shift our focus to a more empirical aspect, interrogating not those who give the order but those who execute it, things once again become more complicated. The cases of Eichmann and Duch also point in this direction. Both of them defended themselves by strongly claiming never to have killed anyone. In Eichmann's words, as reported by Arendt: "With the killing of Jews I had nothing to do. I never killed a Jew, or a non-Jew, for that matter—I never killed any human being. I never gave an order to kill either a Jew or a non-Jew; I just did not do it." Eichmann adds this chilling conclusion: "It so happened . . . that I had not once to do it."[13] Duch would make use of another type of argument, putting forth his intellectual character and his physical weakness. Never, he said, did he risk appearing too sensitive in front of his subordinates, and he was physically incapable of delivering the final blow to the neck of any condemned individual. According to him, these statements are irrefutable proof of his active and personal non-participation in the killings. He gave the orders, he concludes, but he did not kill.[14]

Thus the potential banality of men—their ordinary characters, or even the way their personal abilities are outstripped by their outsized ambitions—does not tell us much at all about other torturers, those who regularly carry out their orders to kill hundreds or even thousands of people. At this level, the banality of evil or mediocrity proves to be empirically almost unfounded, ultimately insufficient for taking account of the participation of millions of men and women in the programmatic killing of dozens of millions of people on every continent, across the globe.

## WHEN ORDINARY MEN BECOME KILLERS

The careful work of historian Christopher Browning helps illuminate the empirical existence of these "ordinary men," or those whose daily existence consists of receiving orders and carrying them out.[15] Through his investigation into a German police reserve battalion charged with killing thousands of Jews in Poland during WWII, Browning is able to provide an exceptional testimony to the concrete structure of these massacres. We learn that these men were in no way predisposed to become killers: Not all of them were young, most of them had families of their own, and all had previously been spared the horrors of war due to their status as reservists. They were no more racist than anyone else and doubtless less ideological than many. Yet they agreed to reproduce the same sequence of actions every day, knowing full well the fatal outcome it would have. They invaded a village chosen in advance for its prominent Jewish community. All Jews—men, women, children, and the elderly, without exception—were immediately arrested and gathered in the village's main square. From there, they were driven by truck into a forest or a nearby field. Without any explanation or accusation, and without any idea of the destiny that awaited them, they were all executed in cold blood upon their exit from the truck. The pressure on these police was on the whole relative; after the first civilian execution, they were offered the choice to be relieved of their duties. Some of them accepted the offer the first time and did not take part in the massacres at all. But by the end of several weeks, all of them, without exception, had taken part in the killings with no other motivation than the *esprit de corps* that united them. Spread over several months, these expeditions alone resulted in the assassination of several thousand people.

Browning is meticulous in his work with the archives of these crimes, collecting testimonies from participants and analyzing personal histories and trajectories through the Nazi death machine. The result of this astounding investigation, still today a milestone, is indisputable: There was nothing at all extraordinary about these men. Unlike Arendt, Browning does not seek to emphasize the mediocrity of these killers through his use of the idea of the ordinary. Or more precisely, he does not set out to track the notion of mediocrity: In the testimonies he de-

livers, it is apparent that some of the men were mediocre, some less so, and others only from time to time. But
this is not his point. In the end, the fact of being mediocre or not being mediocre does not explain all participants' behavior. Ultimately they acted for distinct
personal reasons; they were too different from one another for Browning to hope to find any "common singu-
larity" that would explain their actions in their own
stories, ambitions, or disappointments. Leaving any hypothetical common psychology behind, Browning instead turns to the conditions in which the executions
take place and the social order that commands and le-
gitimizes them. The idea of the ordinary man is simply
a way of saying that the situation is much more important than the prior personal histories of each participant.
Commonly called the "situationist" view, this theoretical perspective posits taking account of the transformation of ordinary men into mass killers using three
complementary registers of analysis: the situationist view
proper, with its inversion of moral norms; the compartmentalization of society, which allows for the division of
populations into entirely hermetic groups; and finally the
submission to authority, which as a principle helps us to
understand the blind obedience of the masses.

According to the first plane of analysis, situations of
power create new "moral" orders according to which new
social norms clearly decree that those designated as
"others" can and should be eliminated. This new norm
gives actors their sense of what is just and thus what

should be done. The general context of Nazi Germany—radical politics, the advance planning and organization of extermination, the hierarchization of tasks, and even the propaganda—promoted the idea of a just cause, making it possible for run-of-the-mill individuals to commit mass atrocity. This is the same thesis advanced by authors such as Herald Welzer[16] and Daniel Goldhagen,[17] even if the latter replaces the idea of ordinary men with that of ordinary Germans in order to underscore the importance of the ordinary anti-Semitism that had already clamped down before the rise of German politics of extermination and which, according to him, greatly facilitated the task of the propaganda of purification.

We find similar ideas in the work of Robert Jay Lifton, with his notion of "atrocity-producing situations."[18] His underpinning objective is, however, very different. For Lifton, the goal is to exonerate the men behind the atrocities and place the blame instead on the war itself—or in other words, on the situation into which the soldiers were brutally plunged and which led them to restrict their ideas of the good to only their brothers in arms and the orders they received. Even if this example did not involve politics on a national scale, and the atrocities came out of a one-time context of extremely high emotional tensions, it is still the case that the mechanism Lifton describes is very similar to Browning's. In each case, a situation overturns the relationship of good and evil and motivates individuals to conform to this new frame of reference, even as they perceive no contradiction with the old one. For these actors, as for the majority of commentators, it will be docility and obedience that best characterize the mental attitudes that lead to the near-passive acquiescence to horror.

If the situationist paradigm stopped there, there would still be the risk that the figure of the monster would reemerge because, if the categories of good and evil are overturned, the difference between monster and ordinary man becomes tenuous, if not illusory. But there is also a second register of analysis, a closer one, although it is less explicit in these first two works. It is most clearly formulated in the work of the Dutch sociologist Abram de Swaan, through the notion of compartmentalization. For him, the internal organization of genocidal regimes—as in many totalitarian regimes—is based on a division of society into tight compartments, in which the fate of each individual is set within radically distinct moral worlds. The distinctive criteria vary from one regime to another, depending on the nature of the ideology underlying the separations: racial or ethnic, in the case of regimes practicing a politics of ethnic purification, political when the ruling class is being overturned and its members curbed or eliminated. The arrangements put into place to effect this societal division also vary widely, depending on the context, whether in terms of the actors who carry out the selection, the restrictions imposed on certain groups and the privileges granted to others, or the places of confinement for subjugated populations (when these exist), and so on—but in all cases this compartmentalization is accompanied by a deliberately unequal distribution of rights and governing rules across compartments. With the exception of those who sort populations into each compartment, who remain the only points of connection between different segments of society, all other contacts are strictly prohibited and subject to punishment. In the case of processes of extermination of targeted populations, no matter what technique is used, the "legal" framework is constituted by the internal ruling arrangements, the chain of command, and the assignments of different agents charged with inspections and surveillance—this is what authorizes, justifies, and orders the killing of all those who occupy the compartment to be destroyed. No one is free to do what they want; each must bend to the ensemble of the rules that frame predicted, possible actions. In the same way, the legal framework that prevails in the opposing container—those who are destined to live—forbids any measure of extermination taken against members of this segment. The only breach of this rule involves individuals belonging to the dominant segment who are suspect or accused of having plotted against the regime—in other words, of having betrayed their group of origin. And it is exactly this betrayal that excludes them from their original segment and puts them in the other segment, in which their execution becomes perfectly legitimate. It is not fellow beings who are eliminated but indeed "something else": a traitor, a dissident, a conspirator, an enemy of the people, and so on. In this way, the elimination of a traitor assumes his prior transfer into another compartment; it is at this price that it does not contradict the rule spelling out the illegality of eliminating members of the dominant group. The political and moral order prove inflexible no matter the segment, even as they are governed by rules and laws that are radically different. The force of their application in each group characterizes the whole of the compartmentalization process.

Thus the killers exclusively target the members of a compartment that has become radically exterior to them. To kill one of these men or women is not the same as killing a peer but, on the contrary, a "being" who is radically different no matter what name they are given. Names like "sub-human" or "Jews" for the Nazis, or "Tutsi" (regularly also called names for cockroaches) for the Hutu during the Rwandan genocide, stress these people's non-belonging to the human world. Compartmentalizing allows for both the putting-to-work of the genocidal project, authorizing extreme violence within the group specifically designated for being eliminated, and for the preservation of the rest of society, forbidding that same violence from being unleashed inside the dominant group. Ideas of good and evil are thus preserved, but in opposite ways in each segment. Compartmentalization allows individuals to commit the most terrible offenses against other human beings without being aware of the monstrous character of their actions—because ultimately they have simply lost the feeling that they are acting against fellow human beings. As we have seen, this is often the line of defense that major genocidaires and their faithful followers adopt.

Yet if this argument is never convincing in tribunals, it is because the situationist perspective—even supplemented by the register of compartmentalization—does not strip individuals of the responsibility they hold at the moment of their actions. This, I should say, is neither its function nor its object. In effect, the situationist view allows for an understanding of the phenomenon as a whole but not what the killers have in mind. The extrapolation from this perspective to individuals' own perceptions of what they do is ultimately pointless. Of course compartmentalization helps us better grasp how genocidal regimes strive to transform humans into other things in order to make them easier to kill. In other words, these regimes put into motion an entire series of steps that pass for ideologies of purification (propaganda, selection and groupings of populations, application of specific laws, naming by non-human terms, all the way up to methodical killing), and these proceed uncontestably from a will to "dehumanize." But the effective realization of this "dehumanization" is an impossibility.[19] As Robert Antelme reminds us, if it is unfortunately easy to imagine submitting men to horrible humiliations, sufferings, and torture, they still can never be transformed into anything other than men.[20] An escape from the human race is impossible. It is always as human beings that people die. Every genocide has attempted to dehumanize, but no matter what terms are used to designate the victims—waste, cockroaches, the impure, enemies of the people, traitors, and so on—not a single genocidaire has ever succeeded in proving that they were killing anything other than a human being. This, furthermore, is the reason why genocidaires kill. Their testimonies regularly converge on the point that they remember neither the faces nor the ages nor the names of their victims—names they had probably never heard, anyways. They all knew, in the end, that they were being asked to eliminate the men and the women no longer wanted by their society. Neither thinking of them as human nor believing that they had simply left the species could have stopped the crime.

Even from the executioner's point of view, this exit from the species is not achievable; and it is certainly useless because murder is all the more easily imaginable when it does not bother with the hypothetical question of the human condition. Ultimately, if the situationist paradigm allows us to understand how a whole society tumbles into a new distribution of good and evil, how it divides men and women into airtight compartments of society, and how it decrees that certain segments are simply destined to disappear, it does not explain why and how individuals agree to take part in it.

## BLIND OBEDIENCE AND SUBMISSION TO AUTHORITY

The third register that completes the situationist paradigm is an attempt to address the question of obedience and submission; beginning with the principle that if ordinary men are liable to become mass killers depending on the circumstances, we can only conclude that there must be psychic and/or cognitive mechanisms that make this possible.

The work of social psychologist Stanley Milgram on obedience to authority[21] is perhaps most representative of the interest in understanding the transformation of ordinary men into killers, which has grown since World War II. In a series of experiments carried out between 1950 and 1963, Milgram and his New York University team of scientists asked volunteers to participate in an experiment that was supposed to test the efficiency of new learning techniques. Officially, the participants were to ask a student in an adjoining room, separated by a glass partition, to try to memorize a series of words and to repeat the sequence when presented with one of the words in it. With each error, the volunteer was supposed to discharge an electric shock to the student using a sophisticated machine equipped with multiple dials and levers. As errors were committed, the amplitude of the shocks indicated on the dial was raised, all the way up to a lethal level. In reality, the aim of the experiment was not to test learning techniques at all; the researcher who accompanied the volunteer was simply a layperson dressed as a scientific researcher, and the student was an actor imitating the effects of electric shock. Instead, the goal was to study the volunteer's reactions (unknown to the volunteer) and to determine at what level of electric shock the volunteer would ask to leave the experiment. The results were striking. In the majority of cases, the volunteers went all the way to the point of delivering lethal shocks without any opposition. Some of them looked questioningly at the white-coated researcher. But it was enough for the scientist figure to let it be understood that the volunteer should continue for them to do so. In very rare cases, the volunteer themselves stopped the experiment before the highest level of shock. For Milgram, the setup was intended to reproduce the prototypical situation of obedience to authority, and the small number of refusals showed the great difficulty of resisting orders, even when those orders were illegal or immoral.

To the question "how does one become an executioner," Milgram contributed to the formulation of an experimental response. In his experiment, any person was capable of blindly carrying out violent acts when a respected authority commanded it. There was no point in invoking fear, perversity, or primal *jouissance* in order to justify such behavior; obedience alone was enough. Milgram's experiment could be seen as the laboratory model that could account for the terrible fall of thousands of so-called civilized men. No particular predisposition—or rather, all predispositions—were liable to lead to the same result as long as authority went uncontested. With Milgram, ordinary man had found its *in vitro* demonstration, which Browning would use in his attempts to add empirical *in vivo* proof. These "ordinary" men are neither monsters nor necessarily mediocre individuals seeking prestige impossible in any other way—nor are they simply cowardly. Here the banality of these poor fools submitted to an experiment beyond their comprehension is not synonymous with mediocrity, as it is for Arendt, but has more to do with their "everyman" status.

Milgram's experiment signals the birth of the conception of the executioner as an everyman. In turn, each "ordinary" man could now be considered an executioner in the making, leading to a proliferation of the scientific—and fictional—literature mixing repulsion for the figure of the executioner with some fascination with the actual killers. Jonathan Littell's novel *The Kindly Ones*, for example, well-acclaimed in France, plays exhaustively on these twinned registers of repulsion and fascination.[22] In the case of Cambodia, François Bizot—himself a captive of the Khmer Rouge before their seizure of power in 1975—has regularly used the same framework to describe the singular relationship he maintained with his former captor, Duch, first in *Le Portail*, which met with significant success. In a later autobiographical writing, *Facing the Torturer*, he sought to penetrate the mystery of Duch's turn to murder, probing the complex interweavings of his torturer's motivations and his own.[23] These types of extrapolation help pave the way for the "everyman" model's success—but they also serve as its principal empirical limit.

In fact, the force of Milgram's demonstration lies in its ability to be both terrifying and reassuring. It is terrifying, first, because it leads us to believe that any and every individual has the capability of becoming a docile executioner. In this sense, Milgram brings a scientific response to the philosophical question of what might transform an ordinary man into a pitiless killer. Obedience, passive submission, the abandon of his inner conscience in favor of the rulings of bosses or authorities: these things, in his view, explain how ordinary men might become the drudges of death. He shows the rarity of those who dare to contest their orders, even when they risk no penalty whatsoever for their disobedience. All of his work goes to show to what point—in a context in which disobedience is severely punishable up to and including death—there would be even less "reason" not to submit to orders.

But at the same time, two elements are implicit in the experiment that could possibly sound a more reassuring note. The first element is the suggestion that, in fact, it would be enough to prepare men never to accept unacceptable (even more than illegal) orders for them to learn to mobilize their own conscience, no matter what authority tried to dispossess them of it. This was the case for certain of the experiment's "guinea pigs," those who refused to slide the lever into the lethal zone. The second hopeful element is much more "philosophical"; it posits the existence of an implicit barrier in "human nature" that would forbid the putting to death of innocent people. Milgram's proceedings stage an experimental model showing the conditions that would permit this "philosophical barrier" to be crossed, without the transgressor knowing or even feeling it. Milgram's entire process rests on the hypothesis that such a quasi-natural "barrier" exists. In fact, the experiment's setup presupposes that the barrier should have driven the guinea pigs to refuse to administer lethal shocks. But if they almost all agreed to do it, this was because the authority present at their sides meant the suspension of their own judgment, abolishing at the same time their sense of responsibility to the point of rendering them insensitive to the other's suffering—and worse, to their death. The explicative chain Milgram suggested stems from this principle: Without responsibility, the executor would not feel what they would *normally* feel under other conditions. The term *normally* is essential here. For once this authority recedes—for example, when the experimenter reveals the setup—the unfortunate guinea pigs realize with horror what they have done and are reassured by the assertion that it was only a trick. The revival of conscience in the aftermath of even a fictitious crime is the most important part of the experiment; it demonstrates that indeed the subjects had not lost their moral sense, or their ability to condemn crime, or their natural repulsion before the killing of the innocent. This is the same principle that caused France to shudder in 2010, after the broadcast of a reality show that more or less reproduced the technique of electric shocks given by an examiner to a fake examinee. Here again, the point was to show ordinary French citizens that passive submission or obedience to absurd orders could have terrible consequences.[24] In Milgram's hypothesis, the natural barrier does exist, but the risk lies in the possibility that its influence could be annihilated under certain critical conditions.

In other words, the problem is that nothing allows us to attest to the existence of this important interior barrier that would necessarily prevent people from acting with extreme cruelty under orders. Already, empirically, the number and the scale of massacres across history argue in favor of the objective possibility of these acts. This is true theoretically as well, since the extraordinary flexibility of social or historical conditions and the near-infinite variety of personality profiles of the men and women who carry out such crimes is not conducive to imagining that in "human nature" there would be a sort of bio-protection against the exercise of violence—not any more than they would lead us to think the opposite, that "human nature" intrinsically contains the potentiality for extreme violence.

In fact, then, it seems to me simplest to conclude that the idea that mass atrocity is connected to the crossing of a supposed interior barrier is ultimately not a question of "human nature." And in fact, if we look more closely at Milgram's experiment, we can contend that this way of seeing the trajectory from ordinary man to executioner by way of experimental obedience has very little to do with the quotidian reality of a functionary in a genocidal bureaucracy. The experiment reduces the environment of the exterminating functionary to arrangements in which obedience and blindness are the only factors at play. In this, it differs in every way from the actual reality of genocidal actors. Of course obedience is part of the killer's reality, but blindness is not. The inaugural principle of the experiment rests on the interrogator's confidence in the authority figure beside them, as well as—or especially—in the appropriateness of the learning protocol, to which they sincerely believe they are lending their aid. Until the end, they do not know that they might have to go all the way to the point of "killing"; moreover, once they have been informed of what they have done, it does not happen a second time. This point marks an essential difference between the experiment's participants and ordinary killers and torturers. When the latter get up in the morning, they know they are going to go kill; no surprise awaits them, no trap is set for them. None of them imagine themselves charged with an educational mission intended to advance the intellectual abilities of their future victims. All of them know that they must kill quickly and well, at best, and at worst, torture before killing. And when they go to sleep, they also know that they will do it all again the next day, and the next, and the next.[25] In the place of the ignorance of Milgram's unfortunate guinea pigs is the perfect awareness of the functionaries of death.

The hypothesis of passive submission thus skirts the question of everyday participation in the administration of death, as well as the issue of the consciences of those who submit to it, killing dozens or hundreds (or more) defenseless civilians without hesitation each day and starting again the next, with full awareness of what awaits and without making distinctions such as women, children, and the elderly. Milgram's experiment will remain relevant above all for what it reveals about the intellectual and moral disarray caused in the west by Nazi barbarism. It attests first and foremost to the way in which western societies have tried to address the thorny question of individual participation in crimes against humanity. To the question "how is it possible that . . . ?," with the subtext that whatever it was should normally be impossible, researchers, journalists, and even lawyers have tried and tried again to find the psychic mechanisms that would explain the crossing into what, philosophically speaking, should be impossible—and yet is not.

## THE PATHOLOGIES OF THE ORDINARY MAN

If mass killers are not all monsters, and if banality and mediocrity are not the only explanations for their acts, and finally, if blind submission to authority is not the determining mechanism in the transformation of ordinary men into killers, what then remains of the notion of ordinary men? The most intellectually attractive ideas are not always the truest, and often they resist any factual proof. The notion of ordinary men is no exception to this rule. In order to preserve its use while avoiding the idea of a destiny common to all men liable to become mass killers in function of the circumstances, certain authors have tried to show that some men, among ordinary men, are less ordinary than others. Two series of complementary arguments have regularly been advanced in support of this idea. The first is numerical; it aims to minimize the number of ordinary individuals who participated directly in mass atrocity. The second is psychological; it attempts to define the psychological and psychopathological factors that would predispose some individuals to become killers.

Essayist and journalist Didier Epelbaum aptly sums up the instinctive indignation behind attempts to find variations among so-called ordinary man. "The idea," he writes, "that we would, you and me, be perfectly capable of smashing babies against walls, is completely intolerable to me. It is the complete opposite of what I am able to feel and imagine. It shakes me to the very foundation of my being."[26] Against the aporia of "all executioners," many authors have tried to support the idea that ordinary men—the "everyman" figure—have never represented anything other than an ancillary force to more professional killers, more limited in number but formidably efficient. Recent discussions on the Rwandan genocide have reinvigorated this numerical thesis, pitting those who see the genocide as the climax of a popular violence involving almost all the Hutu people against those who hold that it was instead the work of small hyper-determined and managed groups who committed the majority of the killings and mobilized the rest of the Hutu population more or less successfully.[27]

According to this view, "ordinary" people represent only a minimal portion of the killers, their proportion having been largely overestimated by the historiography of genocides. The killers would be professionals above all else—seasoned fighters, deliberately recruited psychopaths, or pathological individuals, as we will see variations of in what follows. The vast majority of ordinary men would not be directly involved, especially not in the long term. In other words, the "real" ordinary men are neither victims nor perpetrators, neither resisting heroes nor killers. They have nothing glorious to show off and nothing shameful to account for, to paraphrase the conclusion of Bayard's essay,[28] which offers a way out of the choice between killers or resisters, exonerating the everyman along the way. Yet it is not my intention in this book to engage in an exact tally of active and non-active participants, nor is it to intervene in the controversy over the effective participation of local populations. More modestly, my aim here is simply to underscore the fact that this perspective reintroduces the question of contributing individual factors and of the possibly predictive nature of a certain number of precursory signs.

Despite numerous differences, in the majority of studies the model of the serial killer remains the benchmark for attempts to understand the act of killing as necessarily pathological. The expert psychiatrist Daniel Zagury, who has evaluated the majority of serial killers in France, has developed a psycho-pathological model by which the "pseudo-normality" or "super-normality" of these criminals is their most notable psychopathogical trait, which explains both their affective coldness and their insensitivity to the pain of others.[29] In his framework, the serial killer is a non-decompensated psychotic whose "super-normality" is the clue to his pathology before any action. The act itself can be understood as a sort of terrifying solution that protects the subject from a delusional decompensation. It is in this sense that serial killers are responsible for their actions despite their pathology. But it is also because of their psychosis that serial killers simply do not feel what other ordinary beings ("normal" beings) feel before the horror of their crimes. Applied to genocidaires, this perspective gives an essential role to affective coldness, if not affective anesthesia. It is because they simply do not feel what other ordinary human beings would feel before the act of killing that mass killers can kill without affect, in the manner of the serial killer yet without qualifying as psychotic. For Abram de Swaan, this coldness corresponds strictly to a lack of mentalization that would explain why these men can obey horrific orders without objection and can carry them out without (bad) conscience. It is also the reason why these future mass killers still respect the social interdiction against murder during peacetime but can easily feel liberated from it as soon as social conditions allow. They have almost the same characteristics as every other person in times of peace, with the exception of that much-discussed interior barrier that would render the cold-blooded murder of innocents ethically, morally, and above all psychologically impossible.

For de Swaan, it is also this lack of agency or personal initiative that often leads these men into subaltern positions, always subject to the orders of a higher authority, itself subject to the orders of an even higher one, and so on. Borrowed from psychology and psychoanalysis, the notion of a lack of mentalization has been widely debated in the scientific community as a characteristic of personalities that are admittedly efficient in quotidian life and especially in action, but particularly unequipped when it comes to showing any reflexivity, introspection, or insight. This conception was first described to take account of the psychic functioning of the so-called psychosomatic, those who most easily developed somatic afflictions (stomach ulcers, asthma, and so on) in the place of the anxieties manifested by basic neurotics. Applied to mass killers, the shortcomings of mentalization and operational thinking are directly responsible for the lack of empathy necessary, according to de Swaan, for the completion of the most deadly tasks. "It is by their apparent lack of compassion for their victims that mass murderers are most clearly distinguished from ordinary men," he writes. "It is not possible to feel the suffering of others if it is not possible to imagine what they are feeling, and to feel empathy on their behalf."[30] This failure of empathy does not stem from complete indifference—far from it—but what they feel has no relation to the fate of their victims. Relating the remarks of a former member of the *Einsatzgruppen*, de Swann points out that "he couldn't stand the cries of the children he killed" because they were so loud, and he would certainly have preferred them to die more quietly.[31]

In a more neurocognitive approach, the American neurosurgeon Itzhak Fried has attempted to show the existence of a neuropsychiatric syndrome called "Syndrome E" (E for evil) that the majority of mass killers demonstrate and that would explain the frightening ease with which they kill, without remorse or affect.[32] Following the American DSM classification model for psychiatric syndromes, Syndrome E is characterized by repetitive acts of violence; obsessive ideas of domination and belief in the existence of inferior groups; lack of affect before the act of killing; a sort of mental compartmentalization, separating good and evil depending on populations; a strict dependence of these symptoms on the environmental context of the acts' realization; and, finally, the preservation of all other cognitive and affective functions. Beyond the enumeration of these signs in the standard DSM rubric, the elements Fried sets forth do not differ from those de Swaan describes, nor from what had already been developed by the majority of psychologists and psychiatrists who worked on the cases of Nazi genocide participants.[33]

One more explanatory framework stands to be mentioned, involving the use of psychoactive substances that accentuate sadistic drives, heighten the killers' strength and endurance, and reduce or alter their consciousness of others. In his work *Blitzed: Drugs in the Third Reich*,[34] Norman Ohler puts forth the hypothesis that the majority of Nazi actors were under the influence of powerful drugs (primarily amphetamines) when they carried out their massacres. We find a similar interest in the role—sometimes major—played by alcohol. More measured than Ohler, Browning does not make substance use the single explanatory criterion but rather suggests that the collective drinking sessions held over long evenings post-massacre had a sedative and no doubt exculpatory function, ultimately helping the soldiers to stomach their own daily deeds. The atrocities committed by North American forces during the Vietnam War were also regularly explained by the consumption of drugs, especially heroin, by young soldiers who were quickly becoming actual drug addicts. More recently, an umpteenth version of this thesis of drug abuse by mass killers has surfaced following attacks carried out in the name of jihad. Fenethylline (Captagon[R]), a powerful amphetamine, has regularly been blamed for the violence and extreme brutality of these crimes. Very quickly, Fenethylline has come to be known as the "drug of the jihad"—as the product whose influence is so strong it might explain the way young men were led unawares to extreme levels of violence and even to their own deaths. This claim has been debunked by a report by the OFDT (Observatoire Français des Drogues et des Toxicomanies).[35]

Yet the hypothesis by which drugs and alcohol help facilitate the execution of civilian populations and at the same time offer an exonerating comfort is both too obvious and of too little heuristic value, for several reasons. It is obvious that no one would reasonably doubt that alcohol and drugs could easily be involved in these types of extreme situations. These two products are already very often at play in much more ordinary conditions. But more than that, the association in no way shows causal links between drug use and the possibility of carrying out acts that would otherwise be impossible. No reliable data today exist to confirm any substance use to such generalized degree that it would become an explanatory factor. It is impossible to know if these men consumed drugs to give them courage and to lessen their hypothetical guilt, or if drugs and alcohol acted simply as powerful physical stimulants that let them carry out hard work. I have already emphasized—and will continue to do so in the following chapters—that the execution of a great number of unarmed civilians is a physically taxing task. It is not only a matter of holding down the trigger of an automatic rifle—heavy, loud, burning—for several long minutes; it is not just one blow of a club on the back of the prisoner's neck. Instead, it is necessary to adjust, to warm up, to raise the object, and start over again, tirelessly, for hours. The list goes on. No executioner fails to complain of the physical difficulty of their "work." But this is not all; there is also the noise, the smell, and the cries. Sometimes it is necessary to transport dozens of bodies or to cover up mass graves. Killing, most concede, is not the hardest part—there is still all the rest, the logistics. This is what makes the hypothesis of a sort of break in consciousness at the moment of killing completely improbable. The act of killing is not reducible to the blow of a club or the firing of an automatic rifle or the cut of a knife across the throat. The act of mass killing requires a clear consciousness of all the contingent acts that have to be planned and carried out much more meticulously than the act of executing someone alone.

There are still many shadowy zones in our exploration of the notion of "ordinary man"—far too many for us to place all our hopes for understanding mass murders in this idea. The fact that ordinary men—the "everyman"—might have been less numerous than Milgram, Browning, or Welzer predicted changes nothing, and nor does the apparent discovery that the most motivated or even the most pathological individuals took the lead in carrying out the crimes. Indeed, there is nothing surprising about the fact that those who are most inclined to such violence are not the last to give themselves over to it when conditions become favorable.

For many years, research, commentaries, and defenses have remained focused solely on the ontological conditions that would make an "ordinary" man able methodically to kill others. In thus interrogating the individual capacities of men to commit crimes under certain conditions, different explanations all remain linked to a quasi-juridical approach that depends on the act of killing itself—its motivations or its extenuating circumstances. The act is obviously a crucial instance for justice, for without the act no crime would have taken place. But if we place such value on empirical research into mass atrocity, then we must also note that from the point of view of the actors, killing as such is not the pivotal moment of their existences. Of course it counts, but hardly more than many other moments of the day during which, even if these men are not in the process of killing, they prepare for or carry out various other occupations. Sometimes these activities are related to the moment of killing, especially in terms of logistics; sometimes they have no direct relation, as is the case with eating, sleeping, or moving from place to place, but they retain the rhythms of the killing sessions. In fact, in the quotidian life of a killer, the death of the other is present at every moment, not just only at the moment of killing. This is what must be carefully studied. As I set out in the introduction, it is less important to think the ordinary as an ontological category than empirically to interrogate the *ordinary lives* of those who participate in mass atrocity.

How do these men experience the ensemble of the tasks necessary to the accomplishment of their labor and the satisfaction of their most ordinary needs—eating, drinking, resting, getting around, amusing themselves—on a daily basis and in an ordinary way? This is the question I will address in the following chapters. The ordinary life of mass killers is the key that will open the door to understanding how the administration of death functions on a daily basis. Posed in this way, mass atrocity deserves to be thought of as a total social fact, in the classical sociological sense, following Mauss and Durkheim. It cannot be reduced to the sum of the consciousnesses of those who carry it out.

# 4

## THE ADMINISTRATION
## OF DEATH

Considering mass atrocity as a total social fact means thinking it in all its historical, political, and economic complexity. It also means starting from the individual complexities that make it up. Indeed, it is because without the participation of thousands of more-or-less consenting individuals these crimes would never have taken place that an understanding of the importance of the infamous henchmen of genocidal regimes is essential to a general understanding of the process. Of course, there is the risk that in shifting our focus to these men and their attitudes, motivations, or personal interests, we might end up with a kind of naïve psychologization of the process; the slippery slope into tautology is never far off. But a return to the determining role of the direct participants is not intended to explain mass atrocity. Such crimes cannot be seen as the consequence of some individual craving for extreme violence or cruelty. More modestly, a focus on the participants helps elucidate the social and individual conditions that make it possible for human beings to commit mass atrocities in the first place.

This is an essential distinction and a first shift of our investigation. The theories discussed in the previous chapter all looked to explain why men were capable of killing other defenseless men by the hundreds with no personal motivation. In contrast, however, I now want to try to understand the social and individual conditions that allow these men to be globally indifferent to the deaths of others. Whether we are talking about killers, their accomplices, passive witnesses, low-ranking officials, or the highest authorities, all of them knew that they were participating, that they were contributing in one way or another to the deaths of thousands of men and women. It is this very indifference that characterizes them, although it can take different forms, more or less blunted, more or less active, more or less sincere. But at least one thing seems sure: Not a single one of these men or women made the choice to retreat behind the passive resistance of a Bartleby timidly whispering, "I would prefer not to."[1] I am not referring here to active resistance, nor to a choice for armed struggle. A certain number undertook resistance or struggle, but they are not the ones in question. Out of those who participated in mass crimes, in fact, many of them—with rare exceptions only—could have "preferred not to" without great risk to their lives, but did not. These are still the individuals that constitute the most numerous group. The sum of atrocities committed by more motivated or more indoctrinated participants, or by meaner, more sadistic, or more perverse individuals, will never equal the number of deaths caused by the most massive force of destruction: the indifference of the participants and their accomplices.

Such indifference operates so consistently not just because it is supported by models of cognitive adaptation. Such models do exist, but they prove to be much less useful than we often make them out to be. Manifest in a variety of contexts characterized by the repetition of situations that are supposedly extremely rare or highly anxiety-producing, if not traumatic, this type of cognitive adaptation lessens the perception of the "extraordinary" character of such situations to make way for a form of habituation that makes them psychologically tolerable, or in other words, less traumatic even if still not acceptable. Studied primarily within combat troops, this phenomenon has helped explain why men are able to get used to extremely rough living conditions. Life in the trenches during WWI provides a particularly compelling example. As filth, cold, humidity, violence, fear, anxious waiting, and even the almost constant presence of death came to dominate the soldiers' quotidian universe, cognitive adaptation allowed them to regain a sense of the ordinary, lifting them out of their stupor and returning to them the means of carrying out common, simple functions such as eating, drinking, smoking, discussing, sometimes laughing, and even quarreling.

Yet this example is not an instance of indifference, even if it resembles it. In fact, in the case of war's repetitive horrors, cognitive adaptation fosters a sort of psychic tolerance—a lessened perception of anxiety—but does not necessarily alter awarenesses of what is unacceptable any more than it reduces danger or erases the ethical stakes. Whatever the psyche comes to tolerate via habituation, the conscience still retains the capacity to resist. The kind of cognitive adaptation that works for facing extremely trying situations such as war or extreme violence, and even for getting used to them, is not at all synonymous with indifference. The moving stories of World War I infantrymen, for example, are rife with examples in which the narrator concedes with emotion that "eventually you get used to it," "you make do," or "there was no choice." These statements give way successively to expressions of indignation[2]—or rather, double indignation: indignation at the horror of the war and indignation at having finally succeeded in getting used to it. The accounts of the young World War I soldiers are particularly eloquent on this point. We see how this baptism by fire was a nearly unrepresentable experience in which anxiety—panicky fear, overwhelming and often accompanied by physical and psychic paralysis—translated the horror the novice soldier felt before his absolute ignorance of what awaited him. This initial anxiety, in other words, was provoked less by the reality of battles than by the unimaginable experience that lay ahead. Of course the subject expected to see what he already knew about the business of war, but he did not know—had absolutely no idea—how his body and mind would react to the experience. And yet after this first initiation, as the experience went on, initial ignorance gave way to representations of dangers and increased representability of the emotions that the subject was about to feel. Panic faded and was replaced by fear or worry, as well as the possibility of anticipating effects, preparing for them, or even controlling them so that they could ultimately be overcome via combat, solidarity with brothers in arms, or, for some, the accomplishment of heroic feats.[3]

These accounts have nothing in common with the often-disconcerting stories of perpetrators of mass atrocity. In their case, indifference precedes habituation. There is no inaugural panic; there is nothing unrepresentable about what they are going to have to do; there is no palpable danger putting their lives at risk. There is nothing at all, except perhaps surprise at not having felt very much the first time. Instead, it is over the long term that they become exhausted, as the repetitive gestures, physical fatigue, and disgust as the conditions of executions accumulate to the point of nausea. The members of the 101st Reserve Battalion of German police Browning describes, we remember, drowned their fatigue and disgust in alcohol after long months of killing. But it was neither conscience nor psyche that pushed them to that point. It was much more the case that their lassitude overcame their initial indifference toward their victims.

This is not to contend that these men are simply overwhelmed. Their share of the responsibility is undeniable, as is their culpability; they must all respond to their acts in the courts of justice. But still it remains crucial to analyze the *how* of it, or the context in which this indifference is most generally and most ordinarily expressed. This indifference is manifestly not the product of a cognitive attitude; it is, above all, political and social. Indifference to the deaths of hundreds of thousands of men, women, and children is inscribed in a complex social organization in which the administration of social life is entirely governed by the separation and physical elimination of a part of the population. In other words, a social or economic politics of death reigns supreme, acting as the organizational principle for the ensemble of the prerogatives of those who hold power. This is what the notion of the administration of death helps us analyze.

## TO MAKE DIE AND NOT TO LET LIVE

The administration of death encompasses the quotidian organization of the "life" of all populations—not only the persecuted groups—under a regime's authority. The exercise of its power and the manifestation of its might and its authority are expressed specifically through this general organization by which all quotidian tasks that have any relation to death fall directly under the jurisdiction of the state's hierarchy and administration.

In *The Will to Knowledge* and in his 1978–79 course at the Collège de France, *The Birth of Biopolitics*,[4] Michel Foucault analyzes the historical transformations of regimes of power through two equations that sum up the expression and the exercise of governing regimes. In the era of sovereign regimes, especially in the classical age, the expression of power could be succinctly written as *to take life and let live*. In other words, the sovereign's power was best, if not exclusively, expressed in his superior right to take life: to kill, to execute, and even to torture those he condemned.[5] For others—the rest of the population—the sovereign and his administration had no mandate to make them live or to better their living conditions, whether in terms of their essential needs, their health, or their wealth. This was neither the sovereign's duty nor the expression of his power. The simple fact of letting them live on his lands attested to the strength of his power, and his alone, on their lives.

Following the Enlightenment, the advent of biopolitics in democratized societies was accompanied by the emergence of public hygiene; it allowed for the radical transformation of this expression of power. Now the principal duties of the state and its administration were to make populations they were in charge of live: to assure the availability of vital necessities, to guarantee health, and, in short, to protect the lives of those under its authority by governing. The others, those whom the state no longer wished to hear about, could be let die. The state no longer took care of them—as happens, for example, today, as populations are let die on the borders of Europe in order, supposedly, to protect the lives and interests of European nationals. The strength and the authority of power have no need to take life and no need to kill within their own populations to be recognized and accepted by all. Foucault proposed the phrase *to make live and let die* for this new biopolitics. Still today, this formula sums up the primary organization of the biopowers that govern democratic space.

But when it comes to genocidal regimes, it seems to me that these Foucauldian expressions reach their limits. To be sure, Giorgio Agamben attempted to stretch them to account for processes of mass extermination using the status of bare life,[6] or a life deprived by the ultimate expression of biopolitics of all that makes it social and that is then opened to social, physical, or even historical death. This is manifest, according to him, in Nazi extermination camps[7] or in what he calls states of exception.[8] For Agamben, the Nazi extermination camps represent the ultimate and monstrous culmination of the biopolitics for which Auschwitz is the metonymy.

Yet it seems to me that genocidal regimes escape all biopolitical logics in that they ultimately operate less on bare lives they annihilate than on the lives that they subjugate, eliminate, or spare. It is not *bios* but rather *thanatos* that concerns a genocidal order. The phrase that I would propose to characterize genocidal regimes is the following: *to make die and not to let live.* This formulation has the advantage of letting us situate all the populations administered by a genocidal regime, which are essentially distinguished from each other by the positions that they occupy in relation to this type of regime's sole organizational principle: death. There are three potential positions groups might be able to hold. First, there are the populations that are *made die*: the men, women, and children who are systematically eliminated, whether in mass executions that take place out of sight, industrial killings in extermination camps, simulacra of political trials in security and torture centers, or forced disappearances. Next come the populations that are *not let live*, for whom death remains the only horizon. In deportations, concentration or work camps, and agricultural collectives, there are thousands of individuals reduced to slavery and deprived of all liberty. The regime has no other project for these people than to use them until their deaths. Finally, the last group is composed of the men and women who are spared, and who are neither destined to be killed nor reduced to slavery but whose primary function consists of actively or passively participating in the management of the first two groups. Here we find an assortment of individuals who are directly implicated in the massacres (executioners, guards, bosses, and their logistical assistants), who take part in general administration (from paper-pushers to minor officers of the regime, or those who "do not get their hands dirty"), and finally passive witnesses (who know and who stay quiet or who collaborate from time to time). Although spared, this final group is nevertheless also administered in the name of the same principle—death, that is, not life. In light of this, it seems to me difficult to place genocidal regimes within the realm of biopolitics. They are instead founded on thanato-politics or necro-politics because life is nowhere to be found, not even the bare life that is at the center of the administration of power. In its place is death in its most physical form: bodies, corpses.[9]

The extermination of over a third of the Cambodian population under Khmer Rouge rule between April 1975 and January 1979 is perhaps the archetype of this manifestation of genocidal power. The majority of commentators viewed this genocide as a very particular historical case, if not an exceptional one. According to these commentators, it involved one single ethnic group, and in their view there seemed to have been no exterminating intentionality, just a will to subjugate an entire people at any price.[10] On the contrary, it seems to me that the methods put to work by the Khmer Rouge to execute so many in fewer than four years corresponds very precisely to the basic organizational core that is common to all mass extermination processes. Seen from the point of view of societal organization, and in light of an analysis of the role attributed to each group within the general population, or the quotidian involvement of every person to the point of the life or death of all, it seems to me that the regime established by the Khmer Rouge represents the prototype—the ideal—of the administration of death. In effect, *to make die and not let live* was clearly put into place by the Khmer Rouge. In this respect, a return to the recent history of Cambodia allows for observation and analysis of the quotidian reality of this kind of administration, letting us comprehend the reasons behind the indifference of so many men and women that contributed to its awful efficacy.

## THE KHMER ROUGE ADMINISTRATION OF DEATH, 1975–1979

After five years of guerilla warfare against the proto-American regime led by Lon Nol, the Khmer Rouge entered the capital of Cambodia, Phnom Penh, on April 17, 1975, without resistance. Immediately, the city was emptied of all its inhabitants. Westerners were assembled in the French embassy and were all evacuated to Thailand by truck in the following days. The country's borders were entirely closed and a complete silence fell over what was happening inside. It would be several months before the West would learn the names and faces of those in power. The evacuation of Phnom Penh was, in fact, the deportation of the city's whole former population to the country, where they would be forced into labor. The Cambodian population was thus divided into two groups, the New People, or the "April 17 people"—those who had been "taken" by the Khmer Rouge after the fall of Phnom Penh—and the Old People, who had been on the side of the Khmer Rouge during the years of guerilla fighting. This dichotomy would organize the ensemble of Cambodians' lives during the years of Pol Pot's reign. The New People were literally reduced to slavery, executed in large numbers, and decimated by the thousands by a famine orchestrated under the direction of the Angkar, the powerful revolutionary party organization. During this period, most infrastructure was destroyed, commerce forbidden, property confiscated, money banned, social fabric systematically attacked, previous links of family and friendship abolished, families separated, monks massacred, and so on. In December of 1978, after months of diplomatic tension, Vietnamese troops crossed the border to "liberate" Cambodia. Vietnam set up a puppet government in Phnom Penh, headed by a group of Khmer Rouge who defected in 1977. During the four years of the Khmer Rouge regime, more than a quarter of the population had been killed. Centers for interrogation and torture had been installed across the country, the most famous of which—S-21 in Phnom Penh—was a former school that is today a genocide museum. Mass graves were discovered practically everywhere, but especially close to the interrogation centers where, after weeks of torture, the prisoners were clubbed to death beside enormous common trenches.

The juridical court established forty years later to judge the political and military leaders of these crimes against humanity was first of all a product of the geopolitical concerns that made the Cambodian situation increasingly complicated. The 2001 creation of the "Extraordinary Chambers in the Courts of Cambodia

(ECCC) for the Prosecution of Crimes Committed During the Period of Democratic Kampuchea" was the UN's response to the Cambodian government's demands.[11] This body is a tribunal that is both Cambodian and international, and judges only the primary figures across multiple trials. Trial 001, the case of Kaing Guek Eav, alias Duch, the head of the S-21 interrogation and extermination center in Phnom Penh, concluded in February of 2012 with a life sentence on appeal. Trials 002-01 and 002-02 took place against the four main co-accused—although only Nuon Chea, second-in-command, and Khieu Samphan, president of Democratic Kampuchea, would be judged following the deaths under investigation of the other two, Ieng Sary in 2013, and his wife Ieng Thirith in 2015.

*Recognition of a Genocide in Disguise*

In its press release dated November 16, 2018, as part of trial 002-02 against the former leaders of the Khmer Rouge Nuon Chea and Khieu Samphan, the ECCC pronounced the two guilty of "crimes against humanity, grave breaches of the Geneva Conventions of 1949 and genocide."[12] For the first time, justice had finally recognized the genocidal character of the regime via the conviction of its two still-living leaders. The same day, the French paper *Le Monde* noted the decision, headlining their account—perhaps too hastily—"Khmer Rouge Acknowledged Guilty of Genocide."[13]

In effect, with this sentence, international and Cambodian justice brought to an end a juridical and scientific controversy that had sparked a virulent technical, ethical, and political quarrel for almost forty years, or since the Vietnamese intervention in January of 1979 that marked the end of the Khmer Rouge regime. The question of whether or not genocide had occurred in Cambodia between April 1975 and January 1979 remained dominated by the refusal of some to widely recognize the crimes committed by the Khmer Rouge, and the reserve, of others, about using the term "genocide" to describe massacres whose scope they did not deny but whose genocidal nature they rejected. As an example of the former, the controversial work by Noam Chomsky and Edward Herman, *Manufacturing Consent*,[14] remains a model of the anti-capitalist conspiracy-theory rhetoric that has long served to justify the crimes committed by Marxist-inspired regimes. Their point is not a priori to defend the Khmer Rouge, but rather to denounce Western propaganda methods—the U.S.'s, in particular—and the media techniques used for the Cambodian situation during Pol Pot's reign and up until the Vietnamese intervention. Well known for his work in linguistics and semiotics, Chomsky has also built an international reputation for his militant positions that approach leftist anti-capitalism and anti-Americanism. In *Manufacturing Consent*, the two authors dedicate several chapters to the Cambodian revolution, arguing against Western readings of it. Their argument operates on three levels:

They minimize the survivors' testimonies, relativize the number of deaths, and finally, address the reasons behind the West's questioning of the Cambodian revolution. The first argument thus disputes the reality of the scope of massacres, casting suspicion on the stories collected at the Khmer-Thai border. The argument is classic; it was shared by a good number of intellectuals, including French ones, who saw the first refugees' accounts simply as the result of CIA manipulation. According to the two writers, these exclusively oral testimonies only added a description of suffering, which proved nothing. The stories they contained were always personal, and also "forcefully" manipulated because, on the one hand, these refugees had fled the popular revolution and necessarily belonged to the detested bourgeoisie, and on the other, they probably had to bend to the expectations of their future hosts to hope to obtain a visa in a country of refuge. The second argument attempts to minimize the number of deaths under Pol Pot in relation to the supposedly considerable number of deaths among civilian populations during American bombings—thus before the arrival of the Khmer Rouge—then under the proto-Vietnamese regime after their fall. In Chomsky and Herman's eyes, the figure of a third of the population exterminated in fewer than four years so often brought up across the board to denounce the Khmer Rouge crimes represented instead the simple sum of the three different periods, significantly reducing the number of deaths attributable to Pol Pot.[15] The third argument, finally—perhaps the most essential point of their political demonstration—consisted of putting the "alleged" crimes of the Khmer Rouge into perspective with other mass atrocities committed at the same time, but elsewhere and with less "publicity." According to them, East Timor stands as a perfect example of an equivalent massacre that nevertheless was met with silence in the Western capitals because it served no part of American interests. Thus they argue that certain victims are more "worthy" than others because they can serve the interests of the great powers. The conflation is dubious at best. If the repression in East Timor was indeed bloody after Indonesian annexation in 1971, as more than 200,000 people were massacred, it is still the case that the crimes of the Khmer Rouge were even more numerous—almost two million dead. Above all, moreover, these crimes were not publicized at all during the entire Khmer Rouge period. International media remained silent until the Vietnamese invasion. But once again, Chomsky's target was much less what occurred in Cambodia or of East Timor in reality than a denunciation of the West, twisting the famous conspiracy formula "follow the money" into "follow the propaganda" to find the guilty party. Chomsky and his coauthor directly challenge the United States and its instrumentalization of the "supposed" massacres of Cambodian civilians. To these different ends, the denunciation of American imperialism from the end of the 1970s to the middle of the 1990s was regularly confused with a blind defense of the Cambodian revolution, even to the point of negating the crimes committed in its name.[16] The denial of genocide perhaps remains the best way, in the eyes of such anti-imperialists, to question Western propaganda. Thus, in an astounding *pro domo* defense, Chomsky and Herman concede that it is likely that the Cambodian massacres reached proportions much greater than what was estimated in their book, but they add, self-citing a previous article, "'when the facts are in, it may turn out that the more extreme condemnations were in fact correct,' although if so, 'it will in no way alter the conclusions we have reached on the central question addressed here: how the available facts were selected, modified, or sometimes invented to create a certain image offered to the general population. The answer to this seems clear, and it is unaffected by whatever may yet be discovered about Cambodia in the future.'"[17]

In the case of Cambodia, it is true that on a geopolitical level the stakes were high from the beginning because recognition of the genocidal nature of the Khmer Rouge legitimized Vietnamese military intervention. Moreover, as soon as they had seized power in Phnom Penh, Vietnamese authorities hastened to bring to justice the main Khmer Rouge leaders, who had fled. Pol Pot's co-leaders were charged with genocide in absentia. Yet neither China nor the West wanted to give Soviet military presence in Southeast Asia any new ground. Thus, even if the title of the verdict indicated that the Cambodian people had judged their former leaders,[18] the international community refused to back the verdict—or the trial itself—arguing that the Vietnamese "liberators" had quickly been transformed into an occupying force, losing all legitimacy to represent the Cambodian people.[19] Paradoxically, anti-capitalist militants and Western chancelleries found themselves united against the charge of genocide—the first in order to exalt the revolutionary fervor of the Cambodian successors for Mao Zedong's cultural revolution, and the second to oppose the hegemonic ambitions of Vietnam and its powerful Soviet ally. But in neither case was the Cambodian hell of the Pol Pot years anywhere near the center of their interest.[20]

For others, those who did not deny the crimes committed but refused to use the term "genocide," the argument was more complex and less political, at least at first glance. Using a rigorist reading of the notion of genocide as advanced by Raphael Lemkin[21] in 1944 and adopted by the 1948 International Convention on the Prevention and Punishment on the Crime of Genocide,[22] this argument intends to show, on one hand, that the intention of the Khmer Rouge was not to exterminate a people but to subjugate them, albeit at the price of shocking violence, and on the other, that it was inconceivable to speak of genocide for massacres—whatever their scope—perpetuated within the same ethnic and national group. From this perspective, as for the majority of historians specializing in dictatorial regimes, Cambodia ranks high among the most repressive, and certainly bloodiest, communist regimes, but this repressive politics was not intended to exterminate a population in the name of its religious, ethnic, national, or racial identities, in accordance with the convention's criteria. For these thinkers, the Khmer were killed by other Khmer simply in order to establish the new revolutionary order desired by Pol Pot and his supporters. In this view, speaking of genocide is at best an abuse of language intended to convey that the horror of these massacres should mobilize the international community; at worst, it is a historical error that risks banalizing and perverting the notion of genocide forged by the pain of the Second World War.

But these reserves should not override the arguments made for the denunciation and above all the conviction of Khmer Rouge leaders for crimes against humanity and for the crimes of genocide. From the point of view of these arguments, the stakes are high enough that they deserve to be defended to the point of modifying international law. These arguments can be subdivided into three different claims about what happened: first of all, auto-genocide, or genocide in the strictest sense but with the distinction of having been perpetuated within the same group; next, class genocide, a neologism that sought to make social class a category equivalent to race, religion, or nationality in the general definition of genocide in order to integrate communist crimes; and finally, genocide against specific populations. In this last case, the perspective remains in conformity with international convention and thus limits the use of the term "genocide" to crimes committed against certain non-Khmer populations, such as the Cham, the Vietnamese, or the Buddhist monks who were executed in the name of their religious affiliation. Although this final occurrence on its own was the substance of the judgment pronounced in November of 2018, the two others are still important enough to return to briefly.

*Auto-Genocide*

The primary argument used to refute the term "genocide" rests on the impossibility of imagining that the Khmer Rouge might have gone so far as exterminating its own people. Some thinkers, however, maintained that this actually had been the case simultaneously to underscore the historical aberration that was the Khmer Rouge's program and to characterize the extreme violence—close to a collective paranoia—that took hold of an entire people without the intervention of an "exterior enemy." For these thinkers, the phrase "Cambodian auto-genocide" became, for a time, the means of circumventing the objections to classifying the regime as genocidal. In their view, the fact that both sides belonged to the same people was indeed a dramatic aberration, but this monstrosity did not obviate the genocidal nature of the crimes. On the contrary, their use of the term "auto-genocide" was intended to reinforce the event's monstrous character—an event that, according to them, should figure among the worst horrors of the twentieth century.[23] We also find the term in the work of the anthropologist Georges Condominas,[24] in the foreword to his book on social space in Southeast Asia. In the face of crimes incomprehensible to him as an expert in Southeast Asia, the term "auto-genocide" allowed for the recognition of the scope of the massacre while also exonerating the revolutionary process that had upended almost the entirety of Mainland Southeast Asia. In this way, he wanted to place the responsibility for these atrocities exclusively on a few corrupt autocrats. The term made a reappearance in 1997, following the arrest of Pol Pot and his condemnation by his former partisans until the announcement of his death in April 1998.[25]

The drawbacks of the term, the misunderstandings it engenders, and the historical errors it perpetuates (which ultimately have the potential to result in tragic consequences for Cambodian populations wrongly assimilated to the same identity as their torturers) are widely recognized today. But above all the term ignores the fact that that genocidaires have never needed to establish categories that are based on natural and preexisting ones within populations. It is simply enough for them to declare a segment of the population as other for the whole of the discrimination, segregation, concentration, and finally elimination processes to begin. This is exactly what the case of Cambodia reveals. It is ultimately less of a historical aberration than a characteristic common to all genocidal procedures: Those who lead them never worry about the reality of their categories. The Jews of Nazi propaganda are not the people of Israel but rather an inferior people destined for destruction. The Tutsi of Rwanda in 1993 are not the historical Tutsi but the roaches that *Mille Collines* radio called for to be destroyed. Each of these appellations is first and foremost a construction made by the genocide's leaders starting from categories that they invent or reinvent with the support of a formidable rhetoric that gives them the appearance of natural categories. Thus the case of Cambodia shows how genocidaires are capable of creating entirely new categories (here, Old People and New People) upon which their politics of purification will be organized. At this point, there is no longer any need for such categories to reflect preexisting "identities."

*Class Genocide*

In France, the leading historians who specialize in communism and Nazism often focus on the case of Cambodia. Some of them explore connections with their own research areas; others seek to expand the domain of their investigations into a "brother" country under the influence of an already-communist neighbor, such as China in the case of Cambodia. The 1997 *Black Book of Communism*, edited by Stéphane Courtois, represented the first major attempt at a comparative analysis of the repressive politics (the subjugation of populations to the point of mass atrocity) of the set of regimes that claim a more or less communist affiliation. Cambodia ranks high among such regimes, along with the Soviet Union and

Mao Zedong's cultural-revolution era China. In his introduction, Courtois advances the hypothesis that these regimes are linked not only by a communist ideology, no matter the orientation, but also by their practice of political violence and their ambition to eliminate entire populations seen as resistant to revolutionary ideas. For Courtois, to denounce communist crimes requires comparing them to Nazi crimes in scope and intention.[26] Conscious of the limits of the notion of genocide as previously conceived but still employing the term to gain attention (especially among Leftist intellectuals who still applauded proletarian revolutions), Courtois introduces the notion of "class genocide,"[27] which he borrows from the German historian Klaus Hildebrand, who in 1986 had written that "Hitler's Germany carried out [genocide] in the name of race, the Soviets in the name of class."[28]

Far from widely supported, this notion of class genocide is at the heart of a vast controversy (including among *Black Book* authors) over the exclusively moral usage of the term "genocide." In his chapter on the Pol Pot years, Jean-Louis Margoin, a historian specializing in Maoist China, places the emphasis on the logic of purging established by the Khmer Rouge. Elsewhere, Annette Wieviorka underscores the commonalities between Stalinist, Maoist, and Pol-Potist purges. Rather than setting the Khmer Rouge regime on its own, she also prefers to renounce the term "genocide" and to retain the parallel with the major Stalinist and Maoist purges, even if occasionally she uses it to emphasize the horror of the crimes of the period (but also simultaneously strips it of all juridical signification).[29] Progressively, the idea is established that we must rank the crimes committed by the Khmer Rouge among instances of political violence, purges, and mass killings regularly put in place by communist dictators to subjugate their own people. In this light, the brutality with which the new masters of Cambodia reduced their own people into slavery was perhaps unparalleled, but according to these various authors it nevertheless remained a simple variation of the political violence orchestrated, as elsewhere, in order to establish supposedly communist revolutionary orders.

The ambition of destroying an entire population in order to subjugate it at any price is firmly in keeping with Khmer Rouge slogans, which let it be understood that they were not afraid to physically eliminate all their opponents: "no gain in keeping, no loss in weeding out," "better to destroy ten innocent people than to let one enemy go free." At first glance, then, the classificatory system proposed by Sémelin might still fit the principal crimes committed by the Khmer Rouge against their own people, because the ultimate goal could have been seen as subjugating the Khmer, not exterminating them. The abandonment of the term "genocide" is thus justified by the demonstrated political intention to subjugate the population—again, at any cost—not to destroy it entirely.[30] The fact remains, though, for certain populations also targeted by the Khmer Rouge, such as the Cham Muslim minority, the Vietnamese, or the Buddhist monks, the ambition to annihilate was manifestly present and clearly put into place.

## The Genocidal Extermination
## of Specific Populations

This variation among targeted populations was further brought out by the Extraordinary Chambers' decision to separate the proceedings against the four main Khmer Rouge leaders (Ieng Samphan, Nuon Chea, Ieng Sary, and Khieu Thirith, his wife) into two sub-trials. Khieu Samphan had carried out presidential functions of Democratic Kampuchea; Nuon Chea, second-in-command after Pol Pot, was also president of the National Assembly and head of security, thus directly in charge of repressive politics; Ieng Sary was deputy prime minister and foreign minister; and finally, Ieng Thirith (née Khieu) was minister of social affairs. All four were seen as the thinkers, planners, organizers, and above all decision-makers behind political repression and thus as the instigators of the whole of the mass exterminations. But the magistrates were set on distinguishing in their proceedings between the acts committed against native Cambodian populations and those against certain specific populations. Thus in its judgment on the date of April 26, 2013, the chamber ordered in the first hearing of trial number 002-01 that the four accused be essentially charged with crimes against humanity with regards to their actions against Khmer civilians and the soldiers of the old regime. In trial number 002-02, on the other hand, the same four were also tried for genocide but against specific populations only: The Muslim Cham were systematically persecuted and executed, as were the Vietnamese for their nationality and the monks for their religious beliefs. In so doing, the court applied the criteria of article II of the December 9, 1948, convention to the letter, with its stipulation that "genocide means any of the following acts committed with intent to destroy, in whole or in part, *a national, ethnical, racial or religious group*, as such: (a) Killing members of the group; (b) Causing serious bodily or mental harm to members of the group; (c) Deliberately inflicting on the group conditions of life calculated to bring about its physical destruction in whole or in part; (d) Imposing measures intended to prevent births within the group; (e) Forcibly transferring children of the group to another group."[31]

The court's reading meant the dismissal of some civilian lawyers' concerns, those who argued that the crimes committed against long-standing Khmer were also equally acts of genocide. The court's argument was fair, but it was also insufficiently developed in that the same lawyers had in their concluding remarks argued that the dichotomy effected by Pol Pot's regime between the Old People and the New People immediately after the regime's seizure of power was also accompanied by the New People's unparalleled repression in service of the Khmer Rouge's secondary aim: their physical extermination by a variety of means equivalent to those described in article II of the convention. Thus when, on November 14, 2018, the chamber convicted the two living leaders, Khieu Samphan and Nuon Chea, for crimes of genocide, it did nothing other than confirm the previous precedent for separation set several years earlier. But it did not say—contrary to the surprising media coverage of the verdict—that the Khmer Rouge regime was found guilty of having planned and committed genocide against Cambodian populations.

The particular case of Cambodia had the potential to bring about an evolution of the notion of genocide, providing the proof necessary to denaturalize the categories used in genocides for exterminating populations. Facing a new social, political, and historical reality, one very different than what had been the case when the term "genocide" was adopted at the end of WWII, the international community could have made use of the Cambodian example to show that the Holocaust ultimately represented a particular—and not referential—occurrence of genocide, which itself must be defined more largely to take account of criminal practices that aim equally at the elimination (not only the subjugation or the reduction to slavery) of whole populations. But this discussion never took place.

## FROM GENOCIDE TO GENOCIDAIRES

Thus the use of the term "genocide" has remained tethered to the historical specificity of the extermination of

European Jews, and will probably remain so for some time. But once again, in the case of Cambodia, the stakes of using the term are not to heighten the impact of the crimes committed under the Khmer Rouge, and certainly not to claim any equivalence between the Nazis and the Khmer Rouge. The Khmer Rouge leaders' convictions of crimes against humanity, enslavement of a people, mass rape, and forced marriage sufficiently demonstrate the scope of the atrocities and the guilt of their perpetrators; there is no need at this stage to seek any extra qualifications. But the inventory should not stop there. By refusing to uphold the verdict of genocide for crimes against Khmer native populations, the magistrates introduced a distinction between the different groups persecuted by the Khmer Rouge, even though the practices of selection, deportation, torture, and elimination were vastly similar and included in the same general practices of administering populations and their deaths. It is for this reason, and for this reason alone, that it seems to me important to resist this narrow use of the term "genocide" in the case of Khmer Rouge Cambodia.

Again, this resistance is important first because it shows that the categories used by genocidaires do not necessarily have to have existed before their invention. Indeed, the from-scratch creation of New People was a very concrete way to remove a section of Khmer from the Khmer identity. Through this designation, the Khmer Rouge made them into foreigners, non-Khmer, and above all "waste" to be destroyed, in keeping with the linguistic register of destruction they used. Those who were deported into regions unfit for human life, infected by malaria, reduced to slavery, starved, and deprived of basic medical care until their bodies were finally left to rot into the fields or the rice paddies their peers had to continue cultivating were sent to this tragic end because, for the authorities at the time, they were no longer Khmer. These Khmer did not need to have belonged to another culture or another nationality, or to have believed in other gods, to have been considered not only as enemy but as impure beings whose disappearance would help purify the rest of the Khmer. It was less a matter of subjugating the New People in order to purify them, as Sémelin's categories would suggest, than destroying what in the terminology of the Khmer Rouge ran the risk of making the rest of the Khmer impure. According to the rhetoric of the time, "the New People" "were not really Khmer [. . .] because their minds could not be controlled," not any more than could those of the Khmer Krom.[32] They were "Khmer bodies with Vietnamese minds."[33] This was not about reeducating them, in the manner of the deportations that occurred in China during the Cultural Revolution, but about physically eliminating them so that they did not corrupt the rest of the population.

Next, it is important to insist on a wider definition of genocide because the methods of management and elimination of the different populations considered enemies of power are most often identical, reproducing the same organizational structures, the same sequences, and the same agents. To distinguish a crime of genocide from a crime against humanity has no other import than juridical—and yet. From an anthropological point of view, the methods of execution—like the whole of the organization—that make both categories possible deserve to be analyzed with the same scrutiny. For both crimes, these modes of execution and organization stem from the same genocidal administration of death.

The administration of death first consists of recruitment within groups of the men and women, sometimes adolescents, who are most available to participate in the set of tasks that keep the administration running. At this stage, it is not necessary to find the most motivated or the most ideologically convinced because anyone who is available will do—whether they adhere to the prevailing ideology, whether they are already criminals, whether they hope to profit from their participation, or be protected, or simply to find work. The notion of *the most available* is a fluctuating category, variable depending on contexts, that in no way presumes the pre-existing aptitudes of any individual but is characterized by the facility with which these men and women will accept—more or less voluntarily, more or less spontaneously—cooperation in order to systematically eliminate a segment of the population. The only trait regularly found in these available men and women is simply their indifference: indifference to the fate of those they will only encounter as they make them disappear. These men and women become the genocidaires: killers who kill by rote or who participate in the mass assassination of defenseless individuals only because it has been ordered by others. Their assistants are also genocidaires, as are all the others whose logistical input contributes to the production of eliminating methods and the increase of their productivity. The term "genocidaire," therefore, extends beyond the juridical frame of genocide itself. It also refers to those who are behind massacres of defenseless civilian populations, repeated rape, mass "terrorist" attacks, and deportation, as well as to the guards of populations reduced to slavery, who let them die of hunger, thirst, and dysentery before their eyes.

Genocidaires never, or rarely, invent the tortures to which they subject their victims; they apply them. Nothing more, they say. But this is how they become the essential link in the administration of death. In the following chapter, I will show how their quotidian lives are entirely inscribed into this administration and completely organized around death and the management of death, although without being reduced to the act of killing itself. This act, in light of the lesser amount of time it requires, is not the essential part of their daily lives. Death, however, is everywhere and always present.

The administration of death next consists in the management of bodies—still living or already dead—making them into residues only, matter to be disposed of. What happens to bodies occupies a decisive place in the administrations of death, as essential, if not more essential, than execution.[34] Abandoned, entangled in mass graves or savagely mutilated, sometimes dismembered, burned, destroyed, scattered, recycled into fertilizer, these bodies are regularly assimilated to the massacre's strategic ends—a goal of war, we could say, in the same way that sexual violence not only targets victims directly but aims at the profound alteration of the social fabric through rape as intermediary. In that case, it is a matter simultaneously of taking possession of women's bodies and submitting them to extreme violence, and also of humiliating them, forcing them to bear the descendants of their torturers. In so doing, the whole of the social body is equally targeted. The goal is to obtain complete surrender of all lineages and to abolish the primacy of links between men, women, and the generations to come. It is an identical goal put into the service of an identical genocidal ambition that we find in the treatment of dead bodies. Here, it is the link between the living and their deceased that is systematically destroyed. The disappearance of bodies is compounded by the impossibility of providing any grave or its attendant funeral rites.

In Cambodia during the Pol Pot years, the deported populations were reduced to slavery and worked day in and day out in total destitution in the rice fields, or on vague construction sites, or in the pseudo-hospital outbuildings in agricultural cooperatives.[35] Deprived of food, sustained only by the cooking water from a few grains of rice and sometimes some roots, hastily torn up and hidden from the guard's surveillance, the New

People died systematically of hunger, thirst, fatigue, and dysentery.[36] At least a million Cambodians died before the eyes of the Khmer Rouge and their Old People accomplices. Bodies had to be left where they had fallen; no tomb was tolerated, and no funeral rites. Certain New People risked their lives to provide a simple grave for a parent, a loved one, or simply an acquaintance. Even the fact of placing a corpse in a makeshift rut, dug with difficulty using hands and fingernails, and of covering it with a bit of dirty cloth and a little straw, could lead to certain death if a guard discovered this crude monument. It was forbidden to tend to the bodies in any way, except when the guards demanded they be thrown into mass graves. The message was clear: No longer could anyone count any other person to take care of their fleshly homes beyond death.

This, however, is one of the foundational principles of every human community. The guarantee that human beings be inscribed in the continuum of common experiences rests on the absolute certainty that each person can count on someone—a parent, a friend, a neighbor, the state, anyone at all—to care for their remains. This confidence inhabits each of us, usually unshakably. It makes us believe that even after our deaths, even deprived of all agency over ourselves, our wills can still be heard and carried out. What's more, it leads us to believe that no one would dare to desecrate our bodies, and that the community of the living will guarantee the physical integrity of what we once were. The genocidal administration of death depends on the abolition of this principle. The new principles of the genocidal universe set forth that there will be no such guarantee for the living, no more respect for the dead, no more continuity between generations, and no more sanctuary for collective memory.

Yet every human cosmology affirms the inalterability of the links uniting the living to their dead. In traditional societies, funeral rites, the cult of ancestors, and devotion to the deceased remind the living that before their passing, the dead were part of the same world as the living. In Western societies, we find the same affirmation of this symbolic continuity through such things as funerals, commemorations, monuments to the dead, the preservation of relics, collective memory, and even the search for DNA traces to identify bodies. But all societies across the board draw an impermeable border between the living and the dead to this end: to indicate that they are not of the same nature, that they do not belong to the same category of beings. The radicality of this separation is even more manifest in traditional societies, in which it is thought that the dead are still physically present. Thus even if the deceased and their living can live in the same world, share the same universe and the same system of values, and possibly even meet each other under certain circumstances, they are still never identical. They will never share the same flesh or blood, the same body or the same substance. The affirmation that the dead and the living share one universe literally means that they are necessarily distinct from each other. The dead represent perhaps the closest figure of alterity, but also the most radical one. This constant is one of the foundations of every human community; it corresponds strictly to the idea of social links, setting difference as the principle of every social relation.

The genocidal administration of death deliberately seeks to break this link, effacing the border between the living and the dead. Or more precisely, it attempts to reduce death to nothing other than the bodies of those who are killed or not let live. In abandoning bodies, forbidding funeral rites, and recycling corpses, genocidaires transform lives into simply waste. In their eyes, the dead are never the deceased but only corpses to be destroyed. The destruction process in which genocidaires partake thus goes well beyond the act of killing; it aims at the radical elimination of everything that remains human in the deceased, everything that would evoke any final trace of life. The destruction of bodies is thus an integral part of the genocide process. It is perhaps the most direct expression of the scope and ambition of an administration entirely dedicated to this function.

For genocidaires, death is omnipresent. Even when they are not killing, they must organize all of the tasks that go into this destruction. From the beginning of the process to its end, from dawn to dusk, even if they stop sometimes for a drink or a few cigarettes with their colleagues, it is still death that unites them, death that shapes their companionship. Without death, they would not be together there; without death they would not know each other at all. Each one of their quotidian gestures is marked by its presence. It never leaves their consciousness; even if their minds wander and get lost in futile preoccupations, they know that their days are devoted to all the tasks that go with death. Selecting tools and arms, checking the crew, the transportation, the availability of help—in short, assuring that the logistics are in order becomes the main activity of the ordinary workers in the genocidal administration of death.

Of what—it is often wondered—are genocidaires thinking as they kill? In fact, the response is very simple: of themselves, of course. They are thinking of what they will do or eat later, of the higher-ups observing them, of their friends who are waiting for them. Most of all they are trying not to get injured or dirty. But they are certainly not thinking of those who, in their eyes, no longer exist. An examination of the quotidian lives of these men provides a straightforward rebuttal to the belief that the life of a genocidaire or an executioner or any other mass killer is entirely focused on the act of putting to death alone.[37] All say that killing isn't their fundamental concern; it is not where they take the most pleasure nor where they find the most unhappiness. It is all the rest that preoccupies them: everything needed for the killing of hundreds or even thousands of individuals, the planning of the division of tasks and the discussions this involves, or disputes between colleagues, or of course fatigue and the risk of accidents. In short: the ordinary.

The guards who worked at the infamous Phnom Penh prison were not vastly different from those who were charged with people held in agricultural cooperatives. They were mostly young, only weakly indoctrinated, and lacking both personal motivation and any hatred for their victims. Nevertheless they scrupulously carried out the orders of their superiors—Duch's, for instance, when he ordered them to continue their torture sessions to force even more detailed confessions. But like their colleagues in the provinces, they lived almost in the same places as their prisoners, in spaces requisitioned by the government, in this case barely a few meters from the former school. The urban topography of the set of buildings used for S-21 extended well beyond the main building. There were officers' and guards' quarters, kitchens, refectories, break rooms, and repair shops. Recently, new mass graves, in addition to the ones known already, were found in the school basements and yard, demonstrating that before the decision to execute the condemned, there were already many bodies buried in and around S-21. It was within these walls and these spaces for the administration of death—or an entire neighborhood in the city of Phnom Penh—that these men found one another after work, ate together, listened distractedly to propagandized messages, and slept until the next morning.[38] It was a closed space, exclusively dedicated to the death machine and entirely organized around it. The "life" of these men, if this word still applies in such a situation,[39] still remains ordinary.

If the genocidal administration of death directly produces this indifference among its principal actors, it nevertheless does not exonerate them. They know what they do and why they do it. And all of them put particular importance on accomplishing the majority of quotidian tasks assigned to them with more or less precision. In other words, indifference does not reach into every sphere of their affective lives. Following the example of Duch or Eichmann's defenses, they affirm that their sense of honor drove them to exemplary behavior in carrying out their tasks. In their eyes, they never lost a sense of the good. On the contrary, their sense of the good depended on a job well done, on the rigor and the care they brought to their respect for procedures. The rule and nothing but the rule—the same inflexible rule that required that slips be punished but work done well be recognized. All of them, with more or less enthusiasm, and some with malice, bent to this rule. At least they were not indifferent to that.

This indifference cannot be reduced to a cognitive function. It affects only certain aspects of quotidian life—only the ones that relate to the fate of thousands of people marked to disappear. When the sacredness of life and death are reduced to such banality, then all other quotidian activities rise to the fore, becoming the focus of attention and affects. This is what makes up the ordinary.

# 5

# THE ORDINARY LIFE
# OF GENOCIDAIRES

Rarely have mass killers left precise accounts of their
daily lives. Across the minutes of the major international
trials of recent years—the International Criminal Tribunal for the former Yugoslavia,[1] the International Criminal Tribunal for Rwanda, or the Extraordinary Chambers
in the Courts of Cambodia, for instance—the collection
of evidence, the demonstration of responsibility, and the
presentation of different versions of events, testimonies,
and stories generally take precedence. In short, research
into factual truth orients debate as a whole. Even in the
most detailed analyses of these testimonies, it is the chain
of causes, the different trajectories leading up to the
crime, and the degrees of knowledge and acceptance on
the part of each member of the whole procedure, all the
way up to the premeditation of murder, that are exhumed
in order, ultimately, to establish the level of each indi-

vidual's responsibility.[2] What is uncovered is how each crime is organized, how neighbors come to arrest old friends, how people are driven from their homes and villages, how the spoils are divided, and how entire families—sometimes well known—are massacred. Here the process resembles that of an examining magistrate, seeking the evidence, motives, and circumstances of the crime in its milieu and in recent history. The crime—the act itself—occupies the central place, the point from which personal history is analyzed. Yet if we understand all too well how these men and women become easily used to what they do as they are doing it, still we know nothing about how they live when they're not in the process of killing itself. It is, however, by looking at the manner in which their ordinary lives are also shaped by their functions within the administration of death that we can hope to understand better the *form of life* that makes mass atrocity possible.

Since its formulation in Ludwig Wittgenstein's *Philosophical Investigations*, the notion of *forms of life* has been regularly revisited. The American philosopher Stanley Cavell[3] was one of the major contributors to making it a key concept in contemporary thought, a way to illuminate the enigmatic part of human life as it is entangled with the social and linguistic conditions of individual existence. In essence, a form of life is not limited to the social, psychic, or even biological conditions of life, but it brings together those forms that live through language. This means that a form of life is always conjugated in the plural; it exists as forms of life as they appear in practices, affects, and thoughts, but also—if not above all—in communication between those who share the same living space, words, and grammar of feelings. Language is its principal vector, and it is precisely through expression in language that the ordinary life of the everyday is revealed in all its simplicity and all its worrying strangeness. For the ordinary is also what is taken as acquired, not seen, or otherwise neglected, to such an extent that it can seem obvious or hopelessly banal to us—or more accurately, invisible and unknowable. To apprehend it in all its complexity and immediacy requires the transformation of a philosophical approach to sociology—as Sandra Laugier suggests, for example—in order to overturn this illusory appearance of things.[4] Meticulous analysis of the ordinary allows us to understand what "is just beneath our eyes" and what, because of its physical proximity, usually escapes our knowledge. To return to the ordinary is also a manner of reintroducing the quotidian into our analysis of major events, just as they are revealed to those who live them in the moment or in the immediate aftermath. In other words, it is a matter of removing the historical depth (at least momentarily) that these events will assume later on to approach as closely as possible the manner in which they are lived, spoken, and communicated by those who are part of them—those who are themselves ignorant of all possible later historical depth and act only rarely, if not never, in accordance with it. Their vocabulary is thus never marked by teleological formulas.

This is the main reason that investigations into mass killers and into perpetrators and orchestrators of genocide, like the testimonies and confessions of the accused, frequently fail to capture the contingent reality of human life. For as opposed to what pragmatic sociology can offer as it seeks to understand the quotidian nature of ordinary experience, investigations into the perpetrators of genocide systematically reintroduce historical depth into the acts committed. These investigations piece together, one by one, the sequences whose convergence led to the results we know: the deaths of millions of men and women. This is their objective and how they attain it. But if we shift our analysis elsewhere, no longer focusing on future historical depth but on the fact of each moment's contingency, then we need to take another path and to use other methods. Just as the famous historiographical revolution called on us to make history starting from the ground up, we must now retrace the thread of life back to the moments at which the things we condemn today were accepted, if not valorized.

Again, it is not that those who perpetuated genocide were ignorant of the consequences of their acts and their choices, nor that they could have been unaware of the terrible fate of those who were in their hands. To say that they had no teleological reading of their own lives simply means that at no moment did this perspective come to influence their decisions. It is precisely this point that I want to bring to light. They knew, but their knowledge was in no way a pertinent factor in their analyses of the situation, nor in their capacity to lose themselves in it.

## THE EXECUTIONER

The story of Fernand Meyssonnier, one of the last executioners working in Algiers just before independence, helps shed some light on the daily lives of those whose occupation is killing. Drawing a parallel between executioners and mass killers is obviously fraught, and I want to be careful not to conflate the two. Still, though, both their similarities and their differences are worth looking at more closely. First, of course, the context surrounding the case of the executioner is much less fraught; we speak much more freely about executioners than we do of mass killers.[5] For the former, the fear of penal condemnation is absent; on the contrary, there is a natural degree of official recognition involved. Meyssonnier's book *The Executioner's Tale*[6] is particularly notable for such liberty of tone, above all intended to self-lionize the executioner's own work. Meyssonnier even declares himself disappointed not to have "received the *médaille du travail* or been decorated for devotion to justice. Whereas a pilot who bombards an innocent village," he adds, "runs less risk than we do, and is awarded the Légion d'honneur."[7]

The grandson and son of chief executioners before him, Meyssonnier relates the progression of his career with precision and even a touch of vanity, writing of his trajectory starting as a volunteer beside his father, then serving as assistant and then first assistant, and finally working his way all the way to the coveted post of chief executioner. The chief executioner is the person in control of the whole execution process, the one who makes sure that all assistants are in their places, each one focused on what they must do in the few seconds the execution lasts, and also the one in charge of the final operation of the guillotine. Unlike his predecessors, who were able to carry out their functions until retirement age,[8] Meyssonnier had to leave his post prematurely, at the moment of Algerian independence and the concomitant cessation of executions. This did not prevent him from participating in over 200 executions across his career, 45 of which occurred between February of 1956 and May of 1957—in other words, during the "period when François Mitterrand was the Minister of Justice. Some kind of abolitionist,"[9] he adds, not without irony. Following independence, he was exiled to Tahiti; he returned to the metropole in 1990, but was never to receive another order as an executioner. The account in his book is the product of a long dialogue with the sociologist Jean-Michel Bessette that took place some years after his time in Algeria.

"To be an executioner is not an occupation," he claims, "but a duty."[10] This insistence on duty corresponds to a double mandate for the executioner's role. First, the state prohibits executioners from making the position into a job; executioners do not have the right to earn a living from this post alone. Even if they make a bonus and are exempt from taxation, they must provide for their needs via another form of work—Meyssonnier ran a café, as did his father. This injunction insures the state against too much financial interest on the part of those who enact its justice, at least when that justice is capital punishment. The second factor leading to a sense of duty is that the executioner must carry this massive responsibility with absolute professionalism. Executioners must be both morally irreproachable—disinterested, in other words—and technically impeccable, or professional. Meyssonnier's tale deploys these two figures for duty constantly. "There's no other reason behind putting the condemned to death than to carry out the will of justice," he repeats ad infinitum. He asserts that there is no joy in killing, no pleasure in chopping off heads; there is nothing but the satisfaction of a job well done. A technique perfectly mastered, the tool impeccably maintained, the speed and precision of each gesture, and the meticulous sequencing of all the actors: These things constitute the best guarantee of an accomplished professionalism and its concomitant emotional restraint.

The whole of Meyssonnier's testimony consists of detailed descriptions of the execution's organization, before and after, interspersed regularly with personal and familial anecdotes unrelated to his charge. These detours into the author's everyday world show how he remained simply a man—in the sense of ordinary and well meaning—full of feelings for his loved ones and his friends, as well as for the condemned. Never, he says, should an executioner permit himself the smallest flinch away from the men and women he puts to death. Never can he forget that they are human, just like he is. It is because they are just as human as he is—but guilty in the eyes of human justice—that they must die. Meyssonnier emphasizes that he has no capacity to intervene in the judicial decisions he carries out. He is only the executioner, he admits—of both orders and of men: "If I had to define the role of the executioner in two phrases, I'd say, 1) he must execute orders and not ask any questions, and 2) he must be fast, without roughness, must be human."[11]

But if the executioner is forbidden any judgment of those he kills, or any extra cruelty, and if he seeks to act as quickly as possible so that the condemned has barely any chance to realize that he is going to die after he reaches the scaffolding, he nevertheless sometimes performs certain discreet gestures that attest to greater or lesser compassion, selectively. In other words, behind this affirmation of a simple respect for the decisions of the law, the executioner still holds the power of a relative mercy that he exercises with more or less benevolence, depending on the case. The result is always the same, of course, but the condemned's "comfort" rests in his hands. During certain executions, for example, the condemned are kept away from the scaffolding until their turn arrives. They see nothing but they hear everything: the cry, the clap of the guillotine, then silence. For those who wait, the longer the wait lasts the worse the anguish grows. It is up to the chief executioner to decide the order of executions: The nicest go first,[12] to spare them unnecessary suffering, while the guiltiest or least sympathetic go last, so that they can hear the others' torment.[13] But even before going to this extreme—manipulating fear as a sort of prologue to the sentence—the executioner has the power to control the condemned's last seconds. He is the one who decides how to extract the prisoner from their cell, offer them coffee, handcuff them, accompany them to the scaffolding, and so on. Each of these gestures is influenced by his feelings for the person in his charge. He thus proves to be more or less empathetic according to the case—rough or even rude, if the prisoner inspires disgust or antipathy. In short, he evinces a range of ordinary attitudes, attitudes that would also be found in any other context with less deadly stakes.

The act of killing, then, does not at all sanctify the ensemble of actions that surround it and those of the chief executioner. On the contrary, the quotidian regularly asserts itself. The ordinary dominates each moment of the executioner's life, inserting itself continuously across the different moments of his day. We might make an analogy to managing a business that requires difficult travel: in both cases, punctuality, the necessary upkeep of equipment, and the respect for the client take precedence over every other consideration. All are equally important and are approached with the same seriousness and the same banality, Meyssonnier explains. The same professional qualities are required to guarantee that business goes well and that executions happen smoothly.

This is the executioner's ordinary life. The extraordinary element fades quickly before everything else, as is the case with most things in other lives. The difference, though, is that here death occupies the central place— not simply during the act of killing, but in the whole of the quotidian. Death structures the temporal organization of Meyssonnier's professional activities (café manager, executioner), the maintenance of his equipment (bar, guillotine), and above all his conversations, the language that allows him and his fellow executioners to communicate and to laugh together about things that would horrify laypeople, so to speak, but which their daily life renders terribly banal. For example, Meyssonnier recounts a time the severed head escaped from his hands and a colleague reprimanded him:

> "Stop! That's not allowed. What, do you think you're playing basketball? Magistrates and lawyers are here. Sure, they're condemned but still, have a little respect. At least! Take the head and throw it away, that's it." I said to him, "But you're going so fast, I don't have time!" It was true, I didn't have enough time to dispose of the head in the bin and go back to raise the blade![14]

Or another time, after several executions in a row on the same morning, Meyssonnier remembers that "they could no longer find the body that went with each head, since everything was all jumbled together in the bin." His father then decided to have the prison carpenter make temporary coffins for each executed person "so that we and the prison guards didn't have to look for the head that went with the body after so many executions."[15] This banality is also manifest in the technological progress that allowed the work to become simpler. For example, his father and his colleague, Berger, had the idea to fill the bins for the bloody bodies with water instead of sawdust, "so that they [the bodies] don't stick together and it's easier to clean."[16]

But the comparison with mass killers ends here. Ideology, the magnitude of crimes, the absence of trials, the innocence of victims who are guilty only of existing— of being what they are—and not of a particular action, the exterminators' will to destroy the entirety of the social body all the way up to the memory of the living by disappearing the remains and forbidding funerals, the annihilation of all possible life after their passage: These things belong to a radically different process than anything in the executioner's duty. Even if in Meyssonnier's case most of the condemned were FLN fighters and not common-law prisoners, and no matter what we think about the death penalty and those who work to carry it out, conflating it with mass killing is not justified.

In other words, if I have discussed Fernand Meyssonnier's case in such detail, it is not to suggest that his work is the same as genocide. Instead, I want to show

that even in the extraordinary context of capital punishment—an exceptional exercise, far beyond the norms of
common life and surrounded by multiple precautions
and constraints that lend it an uncontestable solemnity—
the ordinary nevertheless seeps back in. And even without the banalization of each step of the process, the
solemnity of the instant of death could still simply never
be attained. For that, each and every detail of the preparation would have to be meticulously checked not against
the logic of professional habit but of the sanctification
of the passage from life to death. If the quotidian is
thus revealed to be a key element in the analysis of the
killing process, even in a practice like capital punishment that is highly regulated and almost sacralized, the
same thread of analysis of quotidian, ordinary life allows us to study the forms of life in which mass killers
carry out their acts.

## FORMS OF LIFE AND ORDINARY LIVES

For the sociologist Albert Ogien, the concept of *forms of
life* is one of the most powerful tools for describing ordinary reality across very different situations. For him,
this concept can allow us to understand what takes place
even in the most exceptional contexts, outside of all
norms (such as in processes of extermination); it can help
us comprehend the ordinary life of those who orches-
trate political violence. Ogien writes: "If we admit that
all forms of life are coupled with a normative order that

informs what should be said and done in order not to break from the acceptable and to remain intelligible, then killing, raping, corrupting, or lying are normal activities insofar as they happen in a frame which dictates an acceptable manner of carrying them out (by following the rules)."[17] Via this lucid assertion, Ogien points the way toward a deeper analysis of the ordinary lives of those whose quotidian consists of killing. Although this is not the question addressed in his work, which is here focused on the use of the notion of forms of life in the social sciences, we can usefully extend his point into the cases of Fernand Meyssonnier and many others.

Yet with the notable exception of Ogien's remark, which is intended primarily to illustrate the importance of rules in the grammar of forms of life, this notion (like that of the ordinary) has rarely been used to take account of the conditions that make mass atrocities possible and—above all—achievable. Instead, scientific literature tends to reserve these two notions for analysis of the most defenseless, precarious, or vulnerable populations and their living conditions. In the realm of anthropology, Veena Das was the first to reintroduce Wittgensteinian ideas of forms of life to study the long-term effects of extreme violence. In *Life and Words*, she details a descent into the ordinary. Das brilliantly underscores how this notion simultaneously allows us to take account of the immediate conditions of life into which populations are plunged as extreme violence progresses—following the partition of India, for example, or after the assassination of Indira Gandhi—and of the way in which these major transformations upset the quotidian, making way for a different quotidian that then becomes the object of study. The political dimension here is obvious: These different and precarious forms of life are not natural conditions shared by all. On the contrary, they are products of violence, and of the marginalization and subjugation of entire populations. They are above all the direct consequence of a politics of domination, submission, and purification.

In this respect, the notion of forms of life has regularly been used at once to describe the quotidian reality of the most marginalized populations and to take account of the linguistic and practical universes in which these populations struggle. Didier Fassin, for instance, sees forms of life as situations strictly dependent on the registers of representation and assignation.[18] Whether we call them refugees or migrants to qualify—or more often to disqualify—the legitimacy of asylum seekers, he writes, these populations are assigned to live in makeshift shelters, at the arbitrary mercy of state officials. Introducing the notion of forms of life allows Fassin to flesh out these populations' experiences under the constraints of their quotidian. In the case of the unemployed, the homeless, and the disadvantaged of society in general, Guillaume Le Blanc also shows how precarious lives are first of all products of social and political assignation.[19] This precarity is not natural but instead is social—or, more precisely, political. It betrays the way in which these men and women are not only deprived of the majority of the rights due to all others but also of the linguistic instruments that would permit their voices to be heard. According to Le Blanc, the process of precarization that entraps them also reduces their agency, rendering them inaudible to the point of being unable to contest this very assignation or to resist it, much less to actively fight it. Le Blanc seeks to denounce this silencing, returning speech to the voiceless. But this recourse to the notion of forms of life is also a way of returning meaning to these men and women's existences, demonstrating that the ordinary reality of their condition cannot be reduced entirely to precarity alone. The strength of his demonstration and the sociological use of this philosophical notion allow us to introduce the conditions of active subversion—at least partial subversion—into a context of domination.

But if "forms of life" and "the ordinary" are characterized by their relationship to language and to social and political conditions, both take the essence of their heuristic value from their close ties to a specific context of proximity. It is, in my view, this triad that defines a form of life: language, general social and political conditions, and a local context—or, better, a neighborhood.[20] The particular form of life of a group situated in specific social and linguistic conditions is deployed in an area that is limited and often geographically constrained—in other words, a neighborhood. It is because individuals share the same quotidian experience that they express themselves using the same vocabulary, perceive the same objects, and constitute a homogenous group with respect to the form of life that unites them. The real or imaginary belonging to such and such theoretical group or the affiliation with a religious, ethnic, or national group is ultimately much less significant than the incontestable reality of sharing the same living spaces, breathing the same air, frequenting the same businesses, coveting the same partners. Whether these men and women enjoy each other, spend time together, and love each other, or on the contrary detest, hate, or despise each other changes nothing.[21] They live in proximity, in the same world, and share the same quotidian; they are affected by the same things. The notion of the neighborhood allows us to escape from categories that are too broad and too inductive, such as religious affiliation or shared convictions and beliefs, because most of the time we cannot empirically know if individuals allegedly belonging to the same group share all the same things in the same way. Thinking about the neighborhood is the only way to reach this shared quotidian reality that allows us to grasp the ordinary. In other words, it is the "thing" that is present before everyone's eyes. We take it so much for granted that we no longer see it; we think so little about it that we neglect it almost entirely.[22]

It seems to me, though, that the value of the concepts of forms of life and of the ordinary far exceeds the sole frame of analyzing marginalized populations whose "forms of life" are dramatically conveyed by the social precarization to which they are reduced. All situations of confinement or forced proximity deserve study from this perspective—even the most drastic, even when this means describing the quotidian reality of those who inflict the worst violence, the brutalities and humiliations that are authorized by existing regulations. The difference, of course, is that the empathy aroused by precarious, marginalized, or despised forms of life cannot remain in the cases of the forms of life and ordinary lives of genocidaires. Recourse to these notions cannot become a saccharine manner of attenuating the responsibilities of executioners and their aides. Nor should it be believed that such context would "explain" why executioners have become what they are, and nor should we try to find any contextual excuse for these choices by the men and women consciously who did what they did. The stakes lie elsewhere. Ultimately the question is a simpler one: How is the quotidian lived, and how is it lived at different moments of the day? How are colleagues spoken to, meals eaten, rest taken? What is laughed at when the day's main task is putting hundreds of people to death? These things must be described first, before we can even begin to think about interrogating the psychological and/or adaptive conditions that might seem to make these crimes possible. To speak of forms of life consists first and foremost of describing a linguistic universe, a neighborhood, practices and representations. By jettisoning any normative—and therefore moral—*a priori*, we can empirically or ethnographically grasp the constitutive elements of ordinary life. To describe life: these are the stakes.

The potential for empathy is not inherent in forms of life. Of course, the emotion we feel at encountering millions of scandalously precarized lives stems directly from the forms of life that make these lives knowable—lives that are painful, sometimes broken, often mutilated, otherwise ignored. But it is the lives themselves that touch us; their forms of life—the description of their universe, their quotidian lives, the putting-into-words of the radical injustice that affects them and afflicts them—do not make them loveable. In the introduction to *Affliction*, Veena Das carefully and humbly describes the ethical stakes of ethnography: to make the lives she encounters knowable.[23] This descriptive principle corresponds closely with the perspective Wittgenstein introduces, and Cavell develops; it allows for the suspension of normative judgment, making way for precise, neutral—even cold—observation. Emotion and empathy follow, if the observed situation happens to kindle them.

It is, then, indispensable to apply the same principle to the universe of genocide: to make knowable the ordinary lives of men and women whose quotidian is killing, no matter what emotion their acts inspire. The form of life that has evolved in the executioner's case corresponds closely with the definition I have just given. The rules, the demarcation of justice, and the perverted sense of right vs. wrong are not the only things that explain why "killing, raping, corrupting, or lying [can become] normal activities," in Ogien's words—it is also the quotidian existence of an entire neighborhood.

## THE NEIGHBORHOOD, OR THE ELEMENTARY
## UNITY OF THE GENOCIDAL FORM OF LIFE

In *Le Génocide au Village*, historian Hélène Dumas shows how neighborhood relations largely facilitated the Hutu extermination of the Tutsi.[24] Because the killers were already familiar with their future victims, their homes, and their daily habits, it was ultimately easy for them to kill close to one million Tutsi in several weeks. But unlike those who see this genocide as the archetype of intertribal massacre or the paroxysm of an archaic individual cruelty because of this geographical proximity and because of the friendships that sometimes preexisted between executioners and victims, Dumas is able to show that the conception, organization, and preparation of this genocide occurred well in advance, framed by a politics of extermination that was a long time in the making. Indeed, only the implementation was the doing of neighbors; the rest was the result of classic genocidal politics, so to speak. The method changes but not the substance. Thus the transformation of quotidian tools— the machete, notably—into instruments of death attests less to the "savagery" of the crime than to the "professionalization" of killers, who were building from their prior "competencies." These were agricultural workers who were recruited to put the state's instructions into practice with their own instruments and to kill their neighbors, often by machete. At the time, this is what inspired certain commentators to label it a "machete genocide." Following the example of François-Xavier Nsanzuwera, the vice-prosecutor at the International Criminal Tribunal for Rwanda in Arusha, numerous Tutsi survivors spoke out against the use of the term "machete genocide," which introduces formidable confusion between techniques and processes. Moreover, the term establishes a sort of implicit hierarchy of different methods of killing, as if killing by machete is crueler, more "savage," or even less civilized than assassinating with a machine gun.

But the most debate was raised not by the question of cruelty, which is present across killing methods, than by the level of proximity between killers, and between killers and victims. This proximity was regularly the subject of interrogation among historians specializing in the Rwandan genocide. For a number of them, the primary characteristic of the genocide is the fact that it took place above all in a local community—a genocide of neighbors, as some put it.[25] The issue is to understand how people living peacefully with their neighbors,[26] knowing them well, having gone to the same schools, and sometimes even raising families together, could have become pitiless and compassionless assassins. The answers to this enigma remain uncertain. Some thinkers plumb the human soul in all its depths of sadism or cruelty, others focus on the weight of ideology and propaganda, while still others blame old resentments or buried jealousies. Each of these perspectives deserves study, and each illuminates the tragedy in its own way.[27] Yet each rests on the idea—falsely obvious—that "normally" one should not kill their neighbors, and that very particular reasons would be needed—very specific intra-psychic movements, exceptional social and political conditions—to explain how these men could set about killing the people closest to them.

Nothing, however, is less certain. There is, first, nothing "normal" about genocides. Consequently, it seems to me more fruitful to start the analysis from scratch—in other words, with empirical observation, and concomitantly, description. The lesson we should draw from the genocide of the Tutsi in Rwanda is that the fact of being neighbors, and sharing common moments and even families together, is not protection against the violence of genocide. The people who are spared are not necessarily those who are closest to the killers, nor even the most lawful. This is the ordinary administration of death; the categories it establishes replace everything that came before. In this respect, the Rwandan genocide is less a peculiar case of a general genocidal process than one of the most common expressions of that process, albeit an unusually visible one. The crimes committed by former neighbors show that preexisting degrees of proximity change nothing whatsoever.

This is the first general observation that should be drawn about the ordinary life of genocidaires. In the case of Cambodia, the fact that the New People were just as Khmer as the Old People or the Khmer Rouge troops changed nothing in the eyes of their torturers. They were New People, enemies, impure, things to be destroyed and nothing more. Whatever they might have been no longer had the slightest significance. We find the same proximity between the Bosnians and the Serbs living in Bosnia, sometimes with stronger relationships and even marriages, all the way until the beginning of hostilities. In the case of the genocide of the Tutsi in Rwanda, the fact that the Tutsi and the Hutu were old neighbors changed nothing either. It was not as neighbors the Tutsi were assassinated, but as enemies or as cockroaches.

The emphasis placed on the degree of neighborliness between executioners here is a reconstruction by observers, in the aftermath. It has nothing at all to do with what the protagonists experienced at the time. It is this experience of alterity made radical through brutal dehistoricization that must be taken into consideration in order to grasp the ordinary lives of men and women who killed those they no longer wished to recognize as neighbors. It makes no difference whether they knew them before, whether they knew where they lived, or whether they were familiar with their daily routines. This knowledge became nothing other than a strategic element for more effective killing. The better the habits of the "enemy" are known, we might simply say, the easier his extermination will be. It is useless, it seems to me, to seek other specific affects or other transgressions of some higher natural order to account for the fact that the hierarchies put in place by genocidaires to allow for killing simply have no natural legitimacy. Their categories are imposed with no need for the slightest foundation of authenticity, or factors such as religion, ethnicity, nationality, alliance, or even kinship.

The second observation, a more evident one, concerns the recruitment of the most available individuals. This availability, discussed at length in the previous chapter, feeds off a variety of characteristics; here we find all types, from former common-law criminals and idle soldiers to the cruelest and most perverse men to convinced ideologues, the vengeful, and the jealous—and then everyone else, all those who were in no way predisposed to become killers. Whatever the motives that make people available, though, there are at least two elements that are systematically common. Beyond the indifference that lets them feel nothing before the gruesome fates of their victims, also largely discussed in the previous chapter, there is their capacity to come together as a group. They are able to create or maintain a system of relationships—or, more exactly, a neighborhood—in which their shared form of life can take on its meaning. The same vocabulary, the same concerns, the same jokes, or the same disillusions or satisfactions allow the day's actions to become meaningful. Through them, actions and events can be told, shared, and laughed or argued over, as in the case of Fernand Meyssonnier and his assistants. These individuals' attentions are not turned toward their victims but instead toward their companions, their colleagues, their bosses, and their competitors. It is in the eyes of these others that they want to be seen as courageous, respected, even admired. Often they are more cruel than usual—even sadistic—in order to obtain the favor of some boss or another. Of course, in such a context, there is no reason for the most perverse to hold back: This would run counter to sense. The enigma absolutely does not lie in the fact that the most perverse can carry out the worst acts to their hearts' content, though, but rather in the fact that others do the same. Some do it with less perversity, with less refinement of cruelty, or with more mediocre productivity. But they do it all the same. They can do it precisely because the form of life in which their ordinary lives unfold is entirely centered on activities that coalesce around death.

To be sure, hate, sadistic drives, and perverse pleasures exist. They have been regularly discussed by the psychoanalysts who interrogate the perversity of executioners, the return of archaic drives, and the triumph of the death drive.[28] They are frequent occurrences in this closed universe, and they can turn out to be devastating, but they do not systematically have the victims as their object. This is my essential point of disagreement with psychoanalytic readings, which accord too great a significance to the relationship between executioner and victim. This, indeed, no longer exists. With rare exceptions, executioners have no relationship with their victims. The victims already no longer count. Their fate brings no supplemental credit, nor any symbolic or concrete retribution, to their torturers. Besides, the majority of these have no expectation from their victims besides the feeling of a job well done—or at least quickly done—in order to obtain recognition from their peers and bosses; these latter alone count in the eyes of genocidaires. It is in relation to the direct members of their neighborhood—other executioners—that we find those famous morbid drives or jealousies, those little pettinesses or (sometimes) moments of honor that psychoanalysis has shown so clearly to be part of the ordinary life of ordinary neurotics. They look toward their fellows; their expectations and attentions crystallize there.

Even in the case of the atrocities committed in the Croatian camp of Jasenovac during the Second World War, where the massacre of the Jews took an exceptionally cruel turn and culminated in a contest for who could cut the greatest number of throats in one day, it is doubtful that the only motivation for killing could have been to satisfy deadly drives. Even if they were present and largely liberated, these drives were not the only things in play. The practice of a contest underscores this; competition between executioners—whether for the highest score or to obtain the admiration of others—dominates every other concern. The most ordinary passions, such as jealousy, desire, the need to compare oneself to others, or rivalry between killers themselves, are the ones satisfied by expression of cruelty towards the victims. In the universe of death, the victims no longer count and are rarely objects of either conscious attention or unconscious drives. Death and its residues are present, but without the least libidinal investment.

Too often, in other words, we overestimate the libidinal investment of executioners toward their victims but fail to pay the slightest attention to what the killers themselves say. They do not think about the victims, period. They think of each other, of their colleagues, their bosses, their own business—in a word, their lives. Of course they also think about death; they think about it constantly because it is constantly there. But death is not a matter of the living. A sort of thanato-politics takes shape when the whole political organization of the quotidian revolves around death, in a universe where death is always present. In this universe, death is no longer the opposite of life.

The third observation stems from the two previous ones. In the practice of quotidian life, genocidal administration establishes a system of lives that no longer count—those whose deaths alone matter, from the selection of victims to the management of bodies. These practices are founded on the separation of normative registers. Regulations, values, and designations vary, but they always underscore the point to which different groups no longer have anything in common.[29] Moreover, however, vocabularies themselves come to mark out an impermeable border between groups. The distinctions effected by language show the point to which victims and executioners no longer share the same form of life, much less the same neighborhood. The organization of the quotidian serves symbolically and concretely to mark out a radical separation between the pure and the impure, the survivors and the dead. Here again, any former degree of proximity makes no difference; the difference is simply pronounced in the new language of the executioners. Even blood relations cannot stand up to this nomenclature; a Tutsi husband of a Hutu wife is no longer anything but Tutsi, even for his ex-spouse and his in-laws, who do not hesitate to kill him. A son born to a mixed family of a Hutu mother and a Tutsi father risks being killed by his own mother, who no longer recognizes him as a son but simply as a Tutsi.[30] The horror that such acts inspire also reveals the nature of the genocidal logic that declares all prior categories abolished in favor of new ones, which are based on implicit or sometimes explicit principles of selection.

Selection is essential. For all that, however, the principle of selection has less to do with saving the lives that need to be preserved than ensuring the legitimacy of eliminating all others. The majority of the stories and testimonies of torturers all include the same anecdote: A courageous torturer saves the life of either a child or a woman, wrongly relegated to the ranks of the condemned. The visual archives of Yahad-In Unum and Patrick Desbois's team all contain stories of witnesses who are congratulated for having saved one or two lives during the executions in which they participated. For Desbois, the witnesses' insistence on making it known that they had contributed to saving lives demonstrates a sort of guilty conscience, an attempt to make amends through a life-saving gesture, but to me the opposite seems to be the case. These stories instead attest to the much crueler fact that all other deaths were just or lawful in the killers' eyes. This is another example of the principle of selection: by sparing a few lives, certain people can be assured that all the others were "good for killing."

These three observations complicate the widespread idea that sadistic relationships necessarily dominate the universe of killers and their lives. Sadism exists and is widely exercised. It is manifest sometimes with almost limitless cruelty. Sexual violence is the most frequent and most systematic instance of this cruelty in genocidal crimes. But the quotidian reality of those who kill is first and foremost dominated by the physical presence of death and its residues, which structure the substance of each day. It is not their sadism that drives them to live in a universe where it is omnipresent, physically and spiritually, but their quotidian life that leads them to spend the majority of their days with it. In Cambodia during the Khmer Rouge period, or in Rwanda during the Tutsi genocide—as in most places where mass atrocities are committed—genocidaires share this corporeal presence with their victims. They live and they evolve in this corrupted universe. Bodies are present in their conversations; they pollute the water and the soil, working their way eventually into the food supply. And while the act of killing is ultimately so easy for these people, the constant presence of human remains, on the other hand, is more difficult. It becomes the daily stuff of their conversations, their jokes, their frustrations, and their weariness.

This same weariness is what overcame the members of the German Reserve Police Battalion 101, as described by Christopher Browning, shaken by their fatigue and the force of their disgust at killing. The odor of blood and gunpowder never dissipated, even at a distance from the killing sites; the cries of the victims were barely covered by the deafening noise of firearms. Clothes became saturated with mud, grime, dried blood, and encrusted bits of human remains that could not be washed off. Blisters that developed on fingers rendered each new pull of the trigger painful; hands were burned by hot gun barrels or by the constant use of automatic rifles. These are the details the soldiers tried to drown in drinking. But it is also through their drinking that they shared together everything that made up their everyday lives, without any words or thoughts for their victims. They thought about themselves and nothing else. If alcohol was one of the causes of the end of these gun massacres, which were replaced by the industrialization of death in extermination camps, it was not because these men began to be unable to stand killing other men. It was simply because they could no longer tolerate the working conditions that the authorities, fearing a significant drop in the rate of massacres, decided to change methods. Ultimately neither an excess of cruelty nor bad conscience on the part of the killers put an end to the most violent practices. Instead, this was accomplished by weariness and exhaustion.

We find similar descriptions in the testimonies collected by Jean Hatzfeld after the Tutsi genocide in his book *Machete Season*,[31] in Rob Lemkin and Thet Sambath's documentary *Enemies of the People*,[32] and in the film *Graves Without a Name* by the Franco-Cambodian filmmaker Rithy Panh.[33] The men in these works speak first about themselves, their lives, their memories, and their main preoccupations at the time. The chores of the day, and not the fates of their victims, remain etched into their memories. They speak of these things freely— the Cambodian peasant filmed by Rithy Panh, for example, speaks simply and sometimes without emotion of the difficult times he spent under the Khmer Rouge. He seems sympathetic to the living and expresses himself with nuance. He speaks of the Khmer Rouge without hate and has no resentment toward the New People who lived in the region. Besides, the latter are all dead, he adds in passing—giving us to understand that he himself was on the side of the Khmer Rouge. He is no ideologue, even though he says he believed for a time that the revolution would bring happiness for all. But at that time his life was not happy—it was even more difficult than it was at present, and the revolution had brought him nothing. He was never cruel, and in any case cruelty was not favored by his superiors. Efficiency alone was the goal, and it meant exhaustion for underlings such as himself.

We can thus see how emphasizing only the cruelest practices can obfuscate ordinary life and highlight the extraordinary instead. And this extraordinary is so extraordinary that it has nothing in common with what actually produces the most death. In his book *Why Did They Kill*,[34] anthropologist Alexander Laban Hinton surveys a panorama of men who were involved in the killing of more than a third of the Cambodian population under the Khmer Rouge only to return, in conclusion, to the cruelest practices they describe. Distancing himself from overly situationist readings, while also building on Robert Lifton's notion of atrocity-producing situations,[35] Hinton is most interested in the local political and cultural situations that helped unleash limitless and sometimes blind violence. In his view, the Cambodian massacres had to do with ideology, the absence of sanction, and the liberation of tendencies toward cruelty, which were expressed in culturally specific ways. His thesis is neither to situate the crimes in a particular culture, nor to explain them using vague pre-existing cultural tendencies. (On this latter point, he differs from those who, following Prince Norodom Sihanouk, see the Cambodian genocide as a cultural particularity of the Khmer.) Hinton's point is subtler: He shows how the genocide's cruelest practices resonate in Cambodian culture and thus come to bear a symbolism that exceeds the framework of cruelty, although they are nevertheless not exempt from it.

As an example, he gives great importance to the rare cases in which the Khmer Rouge consumed the liver of their victims. As the site of an individual life's force and power, in Cambodia the liver is believed to possess such value that it is often considered a highly prized trophy, starting from the tradition of classical-era warriors. It could be torn from still-living victims and consumed, cooked or raw, both to appropriate the enemy's strength and to prevent him from returning to haunt the living, depriving him of the essential attribute that might otherwise lend him an evil force even after death. In undertaking acts of cannibalism, the Khmer Rouge are seen to have revived this practice. Hinton traces instances of this ritual through the stories of a few of the rare witnesses who, according to their accounts, were very struck by such scenes. The symbolic act is here conflated with its effective realization in a sort of ultimate transgression that is not only recognized as such by the different actors—witnesses and killers alike—but also takes on such demonstrative value that its realization, albeit rare, generates a growing rumor that will be passed from person to person. As horrific as this practice is, in no way does it sum up the quotidian crimes committed during the four years of the Khmer Rouge regime. And even if its legend, from a distance, seems to exceed its actual scope by far, as it becomes sometimes a subject of conversation between the Khmer Rouge and then between survivors, it has never occupied an essential place in the most personal accounts of former killers. This killing practice, in other words, is simply not what genocidaires speak or write of to their families. Instead they recount their quotidian lives: small torments, simple details, lack of amusement, the anger of their immediate bosses, annoyances at their colleagues, and the rare moments of glory when a superior bestowed congratulations or encouragements. These moments are trivial and insignificant; they are of little interest to the grand history of the age. And yet they are essential to these men's lives. This is the ordinary: all that has no historical value in light of capital-h History, yet still takes on such importance for these men and women.

In his book *La Shoah à l'Est*,[36] Andrej Umansky gathers dozens of depositions, stories, direct testimonies, and most important, letters from German soldiers on the eastern front, all of which, only lightly censored, recount everyday existence along the front to loved ones. A few vivid accounts of massacres aside, above all they bluntly and openly reveal the details of ordinary life. Irène Albrecht, for example, a young mail carrier from Wlodawa, passed by the Sobibor concentration camp on her way to work every day. There, she says, everyone knew that Jews were being exterminated: "On one side, mail sorted; on the other, Jews gassed."[37] Mass murder is explicitly included in everyone's ordinary life. Some even hoped to participate in it, in a touristic way, and to be authorized to shoot at least once into the grave where the victims were thrown.[38] Others came simply to look, as they would go to a show or a fair. Everyone knew; no one was alarmed; above all each person maintained the small personal worries that accompanied the massacres. One woman, for example, worried that she might not get back the fur coat she had dropped off at a Jewish shopkeeper's just before their goods were confiscated by the Nazis following their killing. A simple claim letter addressed to her local commissariat meant she was very quickly reunited with the coat.[39] Testimonies to an indifference to death stand alongside declarations of attention or of love, as in a letter from Felix Richard Landau: "It isn't very exciting to kill defenseless men—if they're only Jews. I'd prefer honest open combat. Well, good night, my little darling."[40] In other letters, different quotidian situations are simply juxtaposed in the same light tone: "Today for the first time, we had the prospect of a hot meal. We got 10 Reichmark so that we could buy some necessities. For 2 Reichmark I bought a whip. As soon as we passed the burnt houses, it smelled like corpses everywhere. We slept the rest of the time (all the time)."[41] Still others celebrate soldiers' working conditions and the advantages of their privileged position alongside their commanders. Hermann Gieschen, the photographer charged with "immortalizing" the scenes of execution on film, congratulates himself in a letter to his wife for having "the best post in all the battalion right now. I have nothing to do besides photographing interesting patterns," he says, adding, "And besides, I like the work. I often spend time with the major and the *messieurs* of the administration."[42]

But most frequently, the letters alternate between enumerations of gustatory pleasures regained when packages from home arrived, touristic observations about the villages traversed (and often destroyed), and descriptions of atrocity scenes. Umansky presents a letter from Anton Böhrer, a Wehrmacht soldier, that bears an uncanny resemblance to a normal missive from a tourist to loved ones back home, with the exception that it puts tourist attractions and executions on the same plane. "There's not much to see," Böhrer writes, "since everything has been destroyed, unless you stumble upon an old mansion from the Tsarist era by accident. The neighborhood of American-style skyscrapers is very dull. The cathedral would be quite pretty if the Russians hadn't turned it into a reserve for spare parts. From time to time there's still a building that explodes, where a mine was placed. There are always a few public hangings, of Jews and other riff-raff. That's the only punishment that does any good here. We're supposed to be mercilessly strict and trust no one, even if they look reputable."[43] Umansky's work is full of similar testimonies and demonstrates with almost surgical precision how these men's ordinary was constructed of an alternation between the utterly banal and the death-adjacent, without any emotional separation. In other words, for these individuals, killings were just as ordinary as all the other little things of life, and secondary when it came to their essential place in thought. Across the threads of these stories and these letters, we can see the way surrounding reality is inscribed in this particular form of life. Words match affects, and concerns are the same as they would be under less dramatic circumstances. The drama of those who die occupies no more place than the lack of sausage in daily rations—or even less than that.

To describe the form of life in which genocide operates requires immersion in the interstices of the killers' stories—"along the grain of the archive," borrowing Ann Stoler's words and methodology—"in search of their interests, their concerns, and hierarchies of feelings and sentiments."[44] The story of Kim, a Cambodian refugee who had arrived in France at the beginning of the 1980s, illustrates the troubling nature of these hierarchies. He had come to see me for marital problems. He had been in France starting from the early 1980s; he had remarried in the Thai refugee camp where he had spent several months. His first wife did not want to follow him and remained in Cambodia. In France, like the majority of his fellow compatriots, he found work in the restaurant industry and seemed more or less content. His two sons were well educated. All seemed well, until his wife decided to leave him for a Chinese man (from Cambodia) whom she had met at work. Kim was terribly upset by the situation and could not withstand this departure, which reminded him of his separation with his first wife. She never loved me either, he told me. And yet he thought he had saved her life by marrying her. Of course she had no choice—it was a forced marriage. But at that time, if a young woman who was part of the New People wanted to survive, she had to marry one of the Old People, like himself. He didn't think he was the worst of them. He was former Khmer Rouge, but not an ideologue or a brutal torturer. Instead, he was just a docile executioner, a man who knew how to take advantage of the regime's generosities—to enjoy, for example, a nonconsenting woman. This is how he described his participation in the Khmer Rouge crimes to me: with neither shame nor pride, between two sentences about women. That was a long time ago, he said; he barely remembered it. Yet he spoke to me willingly of his quotidian experiences at the time: deprivation, the lower-ranking officers he was afraid of, although not to the point of fearing for his life. It was a fully ordinary period and nothing more. He felt no guilt, and he was in no way traumatized. You got used to the corpses very fast, he said, but not to the smell, that was all. He had nothing more to say, and in any case he had not come to talk to me about that. The rest was much more important to him—especially his wives—just as it was at the time, ever since the Khmer Rouge had acquired a lovely wife for him.

At the end of the 1980s in Paris, numerous former Khmer Rouge members had found refuge in France. Some were ideologues, former supervisors, or managers, but others were men who were less trained and less ideologically implicated, and all lived alongside former victims or those close to them without outbreaks of violence.[45] The different Cambodian factions present in France had to unite to defend the superior interest of their country against what they all believed to be the Vietnamese invasion. The former Khmer Rouge felt safe in Paris; their exiled government, allied with Prince Sihanouk, still kept the seat of Democratic Kampuchea at the United Nations. Occasionally a few would agree to talk with me about that era, not to confess their crimes— no one was asking them to—but simply to remember the era, sometimes even with nostalgia.

Of course, the majority of the Old People stayed in the country. For most, there was no reason to leave their land, especially because, after the disappearance of the majority of the New People, there was no one likely to reveal them. These minor players were for the most part young adolescents from the country; the oldest among them were likely good rice farmers as well as good neighbors. And yet, without hate or passion, without necessarily any desire for social revenge, and without pleasure, they killed more men, women, children, and elderly than their memory would now let them even count. Interviewed in Guillaume Suon's documentary *About My Father*, one man said he had killed approximately two thousand people with his own hands. But that seemed like a lot, he added. In fact he didn't know how many. He had forgotten the number—but not what he did, of course, because it goes without saying that the gestures and aches of such difficult working conditions are not forgotten: "With a club, you can imagine, it's hard to kill with one blow!" He remembered not a single face—there had been no time to see, much less remember.[46]

Even so, a man in another documentary, Rob Lemkin and Thet Sambath's *Enemies of the People*, remembers his technique for slitting throats with precision.[47] As proof, he reproduces the exact gestures of killing. Without much affect but with excellent muscle memory, he willingly agrees to demonstrate the full sequence, asking an amused friend to play the role of torture victim. Without taking the time to explain to his friend what awaits him, he forces his accessory to the ground, on his stomach, and then buries his knee in his back to keep him still while at the same time tipping his head back by grabbing his hair to expose the neck, hyperextended to suddenly reveal two enormous pulsing carotid arteries. He seizes a small knife, miming a quick and powerful slice precisely from left to right. You need strength, he says, to repeat that all day long. And still at the end of the days his hands gave out; blisters burned his fingers where the knife handle rubbed his skin so badly that he was reduced to simply burying the knife directly in the carotid of the last victims in order to avoid the gesture that gave him such bad cramps. Yes, he remembered the cramps, he says, showing his wrist. Still today, he says, the bodies are all there, not far away, in mass graves that nature has since covered over. No one looked for them, no one mourned them—and he, their killer, knows neither their numbers nor their faces.

Today he has neither hatred nor guilt. From the first, he "had never liked doing what he did." But he did it as best he could, he conceded, "like you do your job under your boss's orders." His boss was a woman who belonged to a party section that was particularly inflexible and cruel; she was unjustly harsh, especially with those who appeared idle in their tasks. He was afraid of her, even if he never thought she would kill him. She had no reason to kill him because he was not part of the New People, but she would yell at him and it made him very scared.[48] When asked what he thinks today about this work, he simply responds that he would rather not have killed so many people and that he hopes never to have to do it again. He seems to understand the distress of his inter-locutor, whose family disappeared in equivalent massa-cres, but at the same time he feels little emotion—no more than he did at the time. He seeks neither to achieve a good conscience by denying the crime nor to relieve a bad one by confessing it; there is no guilt in question.

Fifty slit throats per day, blistered fingers, and cramps in the wrist of the knife-holding arm: Collective history will retain only the first of these things. But from the point of view of the actor, the others are what count and what will remain engraved in his memory. The ordinary story of each executioner does not tell the full history of the event, but encapsulates these men's lives in perfect detail. These two levels—the political history of genocide and the ordinary history of the individual—corroborate each other only imperfectly. The sum of ordinary stories will never tell the whole political history of the crime; they simply describe why and, above all, how each crime was so easy to bring about. The notion of forms of life is not designed to explain why and how certain men become genocidaires. Instead, it allows us to describe their ordinary lives, to represent why this work and these lives were ultimately not as horrifying as they should have been. The only elements that permit a worthwhile explanation of their "transformation" reside in the decisions they made before and leading up to the crime.

Of course these men could have said no to becoming genocidaires. They could have refused orders, escaped, or martyred themselves. But that would not have stopped their colleagues from carrying on. In any case, they did not. The question continues to haunt us: Why did they agree? What would we do in their places? Is it possible to prevent such crimes? Is it possible to get up each day, under threat of life and limb, and say no while the death machine is already running at full throttle? But this is not where the question lies. The ordinary details of genocidaires' lives show that there is not much reason why these men or women would refuse to do their part. Their lives were not at stake and the advantages of their participation were sure. Promotion was possible, and besides, their ordinary life as they participated in genocide was not always horrible—not any worse than life in certain modern industries, at least in terms of salary, if we abstract the nature of production. It is also true that to refuse at that moment would be risky and very certainly useless. As everyone likes to remember: "If I didn't, someone else would—so no use opposing it!"

But what did they do before, before the regime was in place, before the executioners came to power, when opposing their coming did not yet present any risk? When it would have been enough for a majority to have said no to those men and their propaganda? What should have been done before they let them take control of things?

# CONCLUSION

The answer to the question of whether any one of us could become a killer under the right circumstances is absolutely negative. Or more exactly: There is no proof that there is a slumbering killer-in-the-making in each of us, waiting for the first chance to be freed. No more is there a vicious instinct hidden in the depths of the human soul than there are primal unconscious drives that would mean we might all one day become our neighbors' killers out of ontological necessity.[1]

This is fortunate, but it is not enough, for one thing remains incontestable: Certain people will become genocidaires—many people, under the right conditions. The search within human nature or psychic functioning for the reasons why so many men and women commit such violence is long-standing. The hope of finally understanding these reasons feeds in turn into the hope of one day being able to profile future potential participants.

But here again, as I have shown in the preceding chapters, the results are deceptive. The violence of the most perverse, the cruelty of the most sadistic, the resurgence of old jealousies or primal drives, and the passive submission to orders are all present, but the fact that so many men and women who do not show any of these characteristics and have only minimal preexisting reason to commit mass murder are so easily "converted" remains to be explained. Of course, historical conditions have regularly been invoked, and it would be absurd to claim to ignore them here.[2] The general context of various tensions, such as inter-ethnic, religious, political, or national ones, naturally underlies the appearance of infamous more-or-less "hot" zones, to use Alexander Hinton's phrase, which set up entire communities for their descent into incredible violence. The hype of propaganda, the exacerbation of hatred, the stigmatization of the "enemy" and their permanent disqualification through the use of increasingly humiliating terms for them (roaches, waste) or the tattooing of a number on their skins can all be major factors in making the lives of those who are killed even more insignificant than their deaths. At the local level, blind obedience to those who hold power, like the small quotidian arrangements that make profit from the detriment of others possible in any situation, also plays a crucial role. Yet these explanations, even taken all together, are not enough to account for the fact that so many men and women, so different from one another, act similarly in the end.

Across these pages, I have attempted to show that the reasons need to be sought elsewhere, and not only in the act of killing itself, or in the repulsion that this act should "normally" engender in every human being. First, this is because at the individual (subjective) level, the reasons are ultimately more simple and much more varied than we would like to believe. The personal history of each genocidaire is distinct from his closest colleague's, and if each history can help explain *a posteriori* why such an individual became a killer, no single history can tell us why others commit their crimes. No history would fit all imaginable or observable scenarios. But we need to look beyond the act of killing because for these men and women, it is not killing that takes up the essence of their thoughts and actions: Everything else does. The whole of their workdays, in which death is omnipresent in its residues and its preparation, make up the essence of their quotidian reality; death is what they speak about the most. Everywhere they work and everywhere they kill, these men and women spend the balance of their time preparing for their crimes, finding the most suitable sites for them, choosing their arms, selecting their victims, making sure of the contacts they need, and in short, organizing the ensemble of the logistics, rather than reading or learning any ideological lessons. Their quotidian cannot be reduced to ideology any more than it can be reduced to the act of killing alone. It is, however, suffused at every instant by the deaths of others. To live in death is ultimately not the victims' fate, as is so often believed; victims fight with all their strength against death. The victims are resolutely on the side of life and not on the side of survival alone,[3] while the killers exist in death and its concrete management twenty-four hours per day. Even when they are not killing, they are still in death, from the jokes they laugh at to the quotidian worries they share, as they take their meals, over coffee, on their breaks. Who could possibly imagine that these men and women live a sort of split that would allow them not to see what they are doing? They know, and they do it still, even if they take no pleasure from it. They tell their stories with perfect lucidity; they knew they were killing. To live in death—as these men have gotten used to doing—is perhaps no different than any other difficult career. And yet it is not at all the same thing. They do it as they would carry out any other job—in other words, in an ordinary way—yet in no instance are they unaware that what they are doing is no ordinary thing. There is nothing ordinary about killing, even for executioners. This does not, however, prevent them from doing it in an ordinary way.

Since there is no ideology of any kind that, on its own, drives these men to kill, then, two other criteria are also involved, and need to be taken into consideration even more than fanaticism: availability and indifference. Who are the men available in such and such a circumstance? How do they become available, and then indifferent?

Aliza Luft has recently brought to light a certain number of criteria that help us account for how certain individuals sometimes come to move between different positions over the course of a single genocidal process: sometimes docile—or even enthusiastic—executants, sometimes passive resisters, sometimes simply removed and indifferent, sometimes saving several lives.[4] At this micro-level of genocidal practice, it would be effectively erroneous to imagine that each individual's attitudes are completely fixed. They evolve depending on the context, on the mood of the killer or participant; they oscillate from register to register even if the actor is not perfectly aware of it in the moment. Involvement in the crime thus evolves across time, Luft demonstrates, and it would be impossible to try to foresee or predict it. Certainly this is true. But with a caveat, for if the available men can be a little more or much less available at any moment, it still remains the case that at a certain moment they agreed to participate in genocide, in a genocidal form of life— unlike other people, who never rendered themselves available.

The example of jihadist fighters is instructive on this point. The comparison between jihadist combatants and genocidaires rests on the similarity between their methods of criminal action.[5] The juxtaposition of contemporary jihadists with genocidaires who also methodically kill men, women, and children without distinction, in other words, brings out the fact that any similarity has less to do with the ideology behind them than with the methods they use to carry out their crimes. These methods are common to all genocidal administrations of death, and all the men who lend them their support. In this way, the jihadist is no exception, and can be seen as the new avatar for the contemporary genocidaire. The acts of violence that occurred in the towns and cities conquered and then administered by the Islamic State in Syrian and Iraqi territory far surpass the kinds of war crimes that are unfortunately frequent in military battles. In the former's case, mass atrocities are planned and organized; they are destined both to subjugate the ensemble of the population and to eliminate en masse those the new regime no longer wanted. The testimonies I was able to collect from refugees who left Mosul, Iraq, after the arrival of the jihadists all agree, drawing a detailed picture of the establishment of an administration entirely centered on mass death. Civilian populations were selected depending on the criteria set out by the occupiers and resting on a dubious definition of Islamic purity. Even today, after the liberation of the city, the exact number of victims is unknown. Several mass graves have been discovered, and there are almost certainly more, so massive were the executions that were most often clandestine, or in any case rarely public. In the majority of cases, bodies were abandoned in hastily dug pits. Sometimes, though, mutilated bodies were exhibited or hung from the balconies of buildings. The killers were not all the same; they came from different regions and countries and they did not all speak the same language. But they agreed on at least one point: killing and living in a universe where death, present everywhere, seemed neither to bother nor to frighten them.

The massacre of Yazidi populations in Iraqi Kurdistan in 2014 is still the most significant example of this type of genocidal organization. In the summer of 2014, when Islamic State troops invaded Kurdistan, the Kurd fighters, the Peshmurga, were forced to retreat, leaving cities such as the majority Yazidi Sinjar in the hands of the jihadists. Left to the whims of the region's new masters, civilian populations generally were set to be decimated. But it was above all the Yazidi who would bear the cost of the politics of ethnic purification put in place by the Islamic State. Yazidi men were systematically executed; the youngest children were forcibly enlisted and trained under extremely violent conditions to become front-line fighters—to serve as cannon fodder, for some, or to carry out suicide attacks. The women were forced into slavery and marriages with fighters, sold to the highest bidder, or killed, if their torturers perceived them to be too old to serve as sex slaves. Patrick Desbois, well known for his work *The Holocaust by Bullets*,[6] spent several weeks with Yazidi refugees in Iraqi Kurdistan camps to collect the accounts of survivors of jihadist violence.[7] The stories he gathered are horrible, recalling the most extreme practices of the Hutu during the Rwandan genocide, as well as those of Serbian nationalists, especially during the Srebrenica massacre.[8] The mass execution of the majority of men is also accompanied by sexual violence, the scope and systematic character of which attest to the genocidal practices put to work to destroy an entire people and its descendants.

The people available to participate in these massacres are many, whether seasoned fighters who come from somewhere else, young men radicalized in a western country who came to Syria to participate in jihad, or simply "local help," sometimes already involved, sometimes pressured. Their personal motives are equally varied and cannot be reduced to ideological belonging. But all—with the exception of the majority of child soldiers, reduced to military slavery analogous to the sexual slavery of women—agreed to participate in these crimes. All made themselves available to follow the leaders and carry out their plans, no matter what their own personal reasons were. However, even if their number is still considerable today, despite Islamic State military failures, one thing at least is certain: the number of those who should have been available but were not, starting from the very beginning of the jihadist offensive, is much greater.

In the same way, in Western countries the most available men are numerous, found at all different levels of society and varying considerably from one country and one political configuration to the next. All investigations carried out regarding the potential participants in jihad in Western countries underscore the diversity of profiles and social origins, and the great variety of religious and ideological commitments. Ultimately, they find no other common criteria than the fact that some of them, at a certain moment in their lives, found themselves available to "embrace" the jihadist cause. But it remains the case that the number of young people who, according to the criteria established by European authorities, would eventually have been able to be available is infinitely higher than the ultimately very limited number of those who undertake violent action.

In other words, these predictive criteria are not relevant. In the end, they tell us nothing, and in no way do they predict the risk of a "jihadist drift" within a particular population. This argument, too often ignored in contemporary Western discourse, should nevertheless help us target the "at-risk" populations very differently. It shows objectively that the candidates for jihad make themselves available for reasons that are exactly not religious belonging, social position, indoctrination, or radicalization. Of course these factors intervene, but they are simply not predictive of the individual's availability. With the same factors and in similar sociological conditions, the number of available individuals remains very low. The conclusion, then, must be that the most important forces for resisting jihadism and its deterritorialized forms elsewhere lie first and foremost within Muslim populations. In both Western and Eastern countries, they resist the jihadist push most actively and most massively. It is among them that we find the greatest number of young men who would seem to be available but who decided to turn the other way. It is they who, even today, protect the whole of the contemporary world from this border-crossing genocidal violence. Indeed, in light of the scale of Muslim populations around the world, the number of jihadist recruitments remains extremely low. This is the reason for which the Islamic State, like other armed groups that claim the jihadist effort, enlist local populations by force.

Thus, along the stretch of territory that separates Afghanistan from Pakistan, the Taliban and the Islamic State, which are carrying out a war for influence over local populations, regularly conduct raids on isolated homes, villages, and even cities in search of young men to conscript. The jihadists require that families give up their young men to go fight with them. Those who resist are killed; the young recruits are barely trained in combat and are quickly integrated into fighting groups to sow terror in neighboring villages. In these regions far from the front, combat between armed forces is rare; instead, there are sporadic attacks against regular Afghan forces, as well as more or less targeted assassinations of defenseless civilians. It is in order to escape this jihadist "conscription" that boys barely old enough to carry an automatic rifle leave their families by the hundreds, abandon their land, and set off into exile with nothing in their pockets. They are not simply seeking to save themselves, contrary to an idea that is too widespread in Europe. They are leaving because they do not want to join the Islamic State and to become killers. They refuse to participate in a genocide of their people; they do not accept the task of killing their neighbors. These men take the most extreme risks, crossing the east and then Europe, in extremely precarious positions, in order not to be available to kill. The opposite would be much easier. To be available, to agree to "work" for the Islamic State in the region is not very complicated; it is enough to pledge allegiance. Combat is infrequent, and the victims are so harmless that the assassinations are simple and not dangerous. The separation between killers and victims is not even religious or ethnic; selection takes place between those who agree or decide to kill and those who are killed. No demands are placed on future participants in jihad, no eligibility test is required, and there is no proof of ancestral purity to provide (as elsewhere, where anyone can claim belonging in the Islamic State). There is nothing besides a simple pledge. There is not even any need to undergo an intense religious indoctrination—all are already Muslim and possess sufficient theological knowledge, with few variations. Acceptance alone suffices. This is the recruitment of genocidaires; this is how available men are chosen. Nothing is demanded of them besides this availability and that they be capable of killing without any qualms in exchange for a comfortable life. And yet the majority do not agree. This does not mean they are political activists; they resist neither politically nor publicly, and have never belonged to a political party. Some have never even been directly threatened by the jihadists. But they know that their turn awaits, and so they leave. Seen from afar—from our comfortable democracies—these men are nothing other than "migrants" who have nothing to do with the Geneva Convention. Yet the majority of them left so as not to become killers.

When I met Ahmed for the first time during my consultations for refugees and asylum seekers, he believed he was protected by France.[9] After a grueling journey across Iran, Turkey, Bulgaria, and Serbia, he reached Hungary, where he was arrested and forcibly registered as an asylum seeker, with no hope of being welcomed there. He came to spend several months in France under the precarious status granted by the Dublin Accords.[10] But by great fortune, in his words, he had just received the official document from the police prefecture that would let him make his claim for asylum in France.

Ahmed had left Afghanistan two months before the birth of his second daughter. She was now more than three years old, and she did not know her father. When he managed to speak to her by telephone she wouldn't call him "papa," but vaguely "uncle" instead. He cried about it each time it happened. Since Ahmed's departure, his brother had been killed by the Taliban and his mother seriously injured. In France, he had experienced homelessness, the makeshift tent camp at La Chappelle, and now the shelter, where he stayed with several friends as isolated and desperate as he was. But he did not regret leaving; his losses were not meaningless, he told me at each session, repeatedly. He was proud of being Muslim and did not want to become a killer. He was less afraid of death than the dishonor of having to kill his neighbors. He believed that France would give him the right to live with dignity and to send for his family—finally to be reunited with his wife and his children, and to meet his daughter, whose photos he showed me each time to share with me how quickly she was growing up. But the OFPRA (French Office for the Protection of Refugees and Stateless Persons) decided otherwise. The case officer did not contest the reality of his physical suffering, nor even the possibility of links between this suffering and eventual trauma, but he held that these elements did not prove that Ahmed was the victim of direct persecution, and that Ahmed was not at risk of violence on his return to Afghanistan. Moreover, in the words of an interpreter, there were numerous geographical inconsistencies in the story Ahmed had told. The claim was rejected.

"All that for this," he told me. "To make me out to be a liar because a French person has no knowledge of my country and a translator doesn't understand me, to imply that the distance supposed to separate the family farm and the village I come from isn't what I said." Google Maps had in essence trumped his story, he told me. Here was the price to pay, in France, for not wanting to become a participant in genocide. It is incontestable that, for Ahmed, the simplest, the least risky, and probably the easiest choice would have been to join the Taliban or the Islamic State. The easiest choice would have been to become a genocidaire, like some of his neighbors—to agree to kill recalcitrant neighbors, to avenge his brother by killing other innocent citizens, to see the birth of his youngest daughter and to participate from time to time in raids in the name of a perverted Islam. But if Ahmed decided to leave, it was not due to ideology or political conviction. As he said himself, he knew nothing about politics and was not involved in it. He simply did not want to become a killer. This was all—and yet it is a lot.

Ibrahim is also Afghan and comes from the same region. His story is similar. When he was barely seventeen years old, the Islamic State came to forcibly enlist him. He remained hidden for several days to escape them, protected by family members. But the jihadists returned; they knew the family and they knew that Ibrahim was probably not far off. The young men had been neighbors earlier; when they were younger, they had played together, and must have thought that Ibrahim would join them now, as the majority of their former friends already had. There was much less to fear in enlisting than in fleeing, they must have thought. Each day they returned to interrogate Ibrahim's father, mother, and uncles, becoming increasingly threatening. In the end, they placed a bomb in front of the house, killing his two uncles and two of their children. This was when Ibrahim left, beginning the long journey toward Europe through Iran, Turkey, Bulgaria, Hungary, and finally Germany. After more than two years of exile, things were at a standstill. He had also been homeless and had stayed in makeshift tents and shelters; he had hardly any hope of being able to remain in France. He was told everywhere that his story was not compelling enough to obtain the right to asylum. Several days before his appointment at the prefecture to be ordered back to the border, he shared his distress with me again. He questioned his past and his future; he knew he would probably never see his loved ones again. He did not understand why this had happened to him, or why his life had crumbled in so little time because of individuals he had grown up with. One last time, before shaking my hand, he told me that he did not regret his decision to resist joining the Islamic State.

I never saw him again. I do not know if he was taken back to the border or if he succeeded in escaping the police to start a secret life. His fate is unknown, as is the fate of many others. I do not know the exact figure of those who agreed, deliberately or under constraint, to make themselves available to go kill, but the number of Afghan refugees from these regions alone testifies to how many more of them did not agree to save their own lives by stealing those of others. The majority of those I met and who have today lost everything—their families, their friends, their homes, their villages, their country—could easily have chosen to enlist and to become killers. They did not.

Seliman came from another region of the world, Eritrea, where one of the most brutal contemporary dictatorships has cracked down. The country is so poor that there is very little talk of or interest in it. The country's ruler, Isaias Afwerki, has held power since 1993 and has imposed a regime of terror and astoundingly violent oppression. His strength resides in a formidable police force and an army capable of extreme violence against civilian populations. This is not a matter of genocide, but the way in which the police and military forces treat civilian populations resembles the ordinary practices of genocidaires in many ways. Their quotidian is bound up with killing defenseless men, women, and children without trial, with no other reason than having received the order to do so. To this end, armed forces members are subjected to an iron discipline and intensive training throughout their first years of service. Young men are forcibly enlisted at the age of seventeen for an indefinite term, lasting usually until they are forty. Torture is common within the armed forces themselves to maintain order, as well as within the civilian populations, as are mass executions. Like all the youth of his generation, Seliman was enlisted very young. He was taught obedience through torture and privation. Torture was frequent; every minor shortcoming, such as being late to roll call, was punished by several days or even weeks of solitary confinement. Or rather, he was enclosed alone in a simple metal container set in the center of a military field and exposed to the blazing sun and outside temperatures of 100 degrees Fahrenheit, with no light, a single opening to let a little air in, and one exit per day to drink a little water and gulp down a sort of foul gruel.

Like his colleagues, Seliman endured these trials to learn how to obey, and also to kill. The principal object of these trainings was, above all, to harden men into cold-blooded, disciplined killers. But Seliman fled. He found a smuggler to take him to neighboring Ethiopia for several hundred dollars. He was then sold to other smugglers who imprisoned and tortured him until his family could gather the several thousand dollars to get him into Sudan. There, he was again sold to other smugglers who did the same, managing to extort another several thousand dollars from his entire village to transport him to the Libyan border, where he was once again incarcerated and tortured. Each time, photos of his swollen face and bloody body were sent via smartphone to his loved ones to convince them to pay the ransom. The entire village went into debt to save his life, finally paying the last smuggler for his Mediterranean crossing.

When he told the moving story of this voyage, showing me the scars that marked his body, tears came to his eyes. He did not want to have cost his family and friends so much. He knew that they would never be able to repay their debts and would for the rest of their lives be at the mercy of local mafias that would harass and extort them permanently. He would have preferred to die in the Mediterranean, in Ethiopian jails, or anywhere else to spare them. But he assured me that he would never regret leaving Eritrea. He would never become a killer.

Every person who works with refugees can tell stories like Ahmed's, Ibrahim's, and Seliman's by the hundreds. I could have given many more: Syrian activists carrying out the resistance against Bashar al-Assad's regime, leading courageous actions in the diaspora at the risk not only of their lives but always also those of their remaining family in the country.[11] Or still others, like the former Franco-Afghan interpreters who worked for the French army and are today abandoned in the streets of Paris without the slightest official document. The list extends almost infinitely. But with these examples I want to highlight that the refusal to become a genocidaire is not the prerogative of militants and intellectuals alone, nor even of the most engaged in the fight against barbarism. The greatest number come from those who share the same social condition—the same neighborhood, even—as those who are available. This shows the extent to which socio-demographic and psychological factors are very weak predictors. By contrast, within the same groups, ethical positions radically distinguish between those who choose to kill and those who refuse. The men I saw in my consultations described with equal forcefulness their loathing for the killers and their fierce opposition to becoming like them, even if they had to lose everything, as is unfortunately the case today. I also think of a friend, a Bosnian from Croatia, who one day confided to me that at the beginning of the war in the former Yugoslavia he had left everything, and lost everything, so as not to become a killer. He had not wanted to follow the majority of his former friends in deciding to take up arms to kill enemies—but also civilians, in other words, neighbors, often known and formerly liked. I owe him for helping me understand early on that not everyone agrees to kill their neighbor. Not everyone becomes available to embrace a genocidal form of life that is nevertheless still comfortable for those who agree to it. But those who refuse rarely obtain the honor of our nations. On the contrary: We classify them as "migrants" to better disqualify their demands for asylum. It is an ultimate insult for political exiles who never dreamed of leaving their homes. None of them ever dreamed of abandoning their land, family, or friends. When it is not even recognized that they were forced to leave, and when their exile is considered a simple and deliberate choice for "economic migration," they can thus be designated as vile "profiteers" in search of the benefits of a supposedly open and democratic Europe.

To the question that regularly haunts western consciences—"would I have been a killer or would I have resisted"—millions of men and women have already responded. They left. They did not want to kill to preserve the comfort of their lives; they preferred to leave everything. Many of them now rest, anonymous, at the bottom of the Mediterranean. The humanitarian rescue of some unleashes ferocious hatred on the part of governments, on the one hand, and of their people on the other. Others—the vast majority of them—wait in the ramshackle camps at the borders of Europe. And for the rare individuals among them who finally set foot on European soil, they encounter only misery, oblivion, suspicion, distrust, and ultimately a shadowy underground—sad fates, surely, for those who refuse to become genocidaires.

# ACKNOWLEDGMENTS

All my thanks to Rithy Panh, Veena Das, Clara Han, Nilüfer Göle, Sandra Laugier, Fethi Benslama, and Sophie Kecskemeti.

And to Ann Stoler, Miriam Ticktin, Stéphane Audoin Rouzeau, Georges Vigarello, Frédérique Matonti, Jean Frédéric Schaub, Deborah Furet, Lotte Buch Segal, and my colleagues at CESPRA and LabEx Tepsis.

Thank you to Blandine Genthon for having welcomed this project and this book into CNRS Editions from the beginning, and for guiding it with enthusiasm and patience.

Thank you to Thomas Lay for welcoming this book at Fordham University Press.

And a very special thanks to Lindsay Turner for her remarkable work on the translation of this book.

And of course thank you to Vannina, Julia, and Paola.

# NOTES

**INTRODUCTION**

1. Jacques Sémelin, "Introduction: Violences Extrêmes: Peut-on Comprendre?" *Revue Internationale des Sciences Sociales* 4, no. 174 (2002): 479–81.

2. Jacques Sémelin, "Du Massacre au Processus Génocidaire," *Revue Internationale des Sciences Sociales* 4, no. 174 (2002): 483–92.

3. Jacques Sémelin, *Purify and Destroy: The Political Uses of Massacre and Genocide*, trans. Cynthia Schoch (New York: Columbia University Press, 2007).

4. Michaël Prazan, *Einsatzgruppen: Sur les Traces des Commandos de la Mort Nazis* (Paris: Seuil, 2013).

5. Daniel Zagury, *La Barbarie des Hommes Ordinaires* (Paris: Editions de l'Observatoire, 2018).

6. Veena Das, *Life and Words: Violence and the Descent into the Ordinary* (Berkeley: University of California Press, 2007).

1. See David Chandler, *Brother Number One: A Political Biography of Pol Pot* (Boulder, Colo.: Westview Press, 1999).

2. Chea died in prison in Phnom Penh on August 4, 2019.

3. See Chapter 4.

4. Thierry Cruvellier, *Le Maître des Aveux* (Paris: Gallimard, 2011).

5. Rithy Panh, *Duch: Master of the Forges of Hell* (New York: First Run Features, 2011), film.

6. Richard Rechtman, "Reconstitution de la Scène du Crime: à Propos de Duch, le Mâtre des Forges de Rithy Panh," *Etudes, Revue de Culture Contemporaine*, July (4154) 2011: 320–39.

7. Rithy Panh, *Duch*, 2011.

8. Joshua Oppenheimer, *The Act of Killing* (Copenhagen: Final Cut for Real, 2012), film.

9. See Jean Hatzfeld, *Machete Season: The Killers in Rwanda Speak*, trans. Linda Coverdale (New York: FSG, 2006), as well as Hélène Dumas, *Le Genocide au Village: le Massacre des Tutsi du Rwanda* (Paris: Seuil, 2014), and Stéphane Audoin-Rouzeau, *Une Initiation: Rwanda 1994–2016* (Paris: Seuil, 2017).

10. Claude Lanzmann's *Shoah* might be seen as the prototype of these types of documentaries, which work to bring the killers' words to light.

11. http://law2.umkc.edu/faculty/projects/ftrials/mylai/myl_Calltest.html.

12. For details on the My Lai massacre and its influence on American collective memory, see Allan Young, *The Harmony of Illusions: Inventing Post-Traumatic Stress Disorder* (Princeton: Princeton University Press, 1995) as well as Didier Fassin and Richard Rechtman, *The Empire of Trauma: An Inquiry into the Condition of Victimhood*, trans. Rachel Gomme (Princeton: Princeton University Press, 2009).

13. At the time, the VVAW was the most powerful veterans association fiercely engaged against the war and for the end of combat. Its members included lower-ranking soldiers as well as decorated heroes, such as John Kerry.

14. Vietnam Veterans Against the War, *The Winter Soldier Investigation: An Inquiry into American War Crimes* (Boston: Beacon Press, 1972). See also *Winter Soldier*, a documentary about the event.

15. See Richard Rechtman, "Mémoire et Anthropologie: le Traumatisme Comme Invention Sociale," in *Les Chantiers de la Memoire*, ed. Maréchal D. Peschanski (Bry Sur Marne: INA Editions, 2013), 98–114, for the way in which atrocities committed during the Vietnam War influence conceptions of memory and modern war.

16. Robert Jay Lifton, *Death in Life: Survivors of Hiroshima* (Chapel Hill: University of North Carolina Press, 1968).

17. Later, he would fight with the same passion against the death penalty in the United States, and more recently against President Donald Trump.

18. The term given to American soldiers involved in these atrocities (which included the murder of children) by opponents to the Vietnam War, an effect partially produced by Nick Ut's famous "napalm girl" photo.

19. Robert Lifton, *Home From the War: Learning from Vietnam Veterans* (Boston: Beacon Press, 1973).

20. https://www.icty.org/en/content/miroslav-bralo.

21. For example, consider the injunctions broadcast on *Mille Collines* radio during the Rwandan genocide, constantly affirming the necessity and the virtuousness of crimes against Tutsi civilians.

22. Of notable exception are the Indonesian torturers filmed by Joshua Oppenheimer, who still today take pleasure in seeming to be bloodthirsty monsters (I will return to this point).

## 2. MONSTERS: CRUELTY AND *JOUISSANCE*

1. See Stéphane Audoin-Rouzeau, *Combattre: Une Anthropologie Historique de la Guerre Moderne, XIX–XXIe Siècle* (Paris: Seuil, 2008).

2. See, for example, Wes Williams, *Monsters and Their Meanings in Early Modern Culture: Mighty Magic* (Oxford: Oxford University Press, 2011).

3. See Marc Renneville, *Crime et Folie: Deux Siècles d'Enquêtes Médicales et Judiciaires* (Paris: Fayard, 2003).

4. We will see further on how this dubious assimilation has regularly been exploited in certain contemporary

literary writings, turning the killer into a simple victim of their circumstances. For a vigorous deconstruction of this tendency, see Charlotte Lacoste, *Séductions du Bourreau: Négation des Victimes* (Paris: PUF, 2010).

5. See Pierre Bayard's daring auto-fictional/biographical essay, *Aurai-je été résistant ou bourreau?* (Paris: Seuil, 2013).

6. At the date of the play's production, in July 2016, the fear of a National Front victory in the French presidential election of 2017 was ever more pressing, to the point that the majority of commentators ventured to imagine the scenario concretely.

7. Abraham de Swaan, *Diviser Pour Tuer: Les Régimes Génocidaires et Leurs Hommes de Main* (Paris: Seuil, 2016). See also Chapter 4.

8. Norbert Elias, *The History of Manners (The Civilizing Process, Vol. 1)* (New York: Pantheon, 1982).

9. See Roger Chartier, "Barbarie et Décivilisation: Preface," in Norbert Elias, *Les Allemands: Evolution des Habitus et Lutte de Pouvoir aux XIX et XXe Siècles* (Paris: Seuil, 2017).

10. Norbert Elias, *Les Allemands: Evolution des Habitus et Lutte de Pouvoir aux XIX et XXe Siècles* (Paris: Seuil, 2017). See also Sabine Delzescaux's excellent analysis in *Norbert Elias: Distinction, Conscience, et Violence* (Paris: Armand Colin, 2016).

11. Pierre Bayard, *Aurai-Je Éte Résistant ou Bourreau?* (Paris: Les Éditions de Minuit, 2013), 13.

12. See, for example, Pierre Bayard, *How to Talk About Books You Haven't Read*, trans. Jeffrey Mehlman (New York: Bloomsbury, 2009).

13. This hypothetical proximity with the killers of the Second World War and their collaborators is worth contrasting with the resurgence of the figure of the radically other monster, associated with the killers taking part in Islamic jihad.

14. Pierre Bayard, *Aurai-Je*, 17.

15. Let us note in passing that the clemency recommended by these good people is above all else a sort of anticipatory demand for clemency for themselves, if one day they happen to find themselves in the killers' places. Brilliantly denounced in its literary form by Charlotte Lacoste (*Seductions*, 2014), this appeal of the killer is unfortunately not limited only to writers. In Cambodia, for example, at the very beginning of Duch's first trial, I was assailed by Western journalists and heads of NGOs regarding my opinions and my writings in favor of proceedings against the minor players—those whose quotidian was killing—as well as against those who organized genocide. The argument was always the same: These men were not responsible for their acts; they were simply obeying orders; they had decided nothing themselves, and in any case they had had no choice. This last argument always came last. Of course. But this is not the only instance in which a crime, a misdemeanor, or a simple transgression has been committed by an individual who might not have had any other choice. For

example, let's say the driver of a car runs over a pedestrian while swerving to avoid another vehicle. Certainly there was no other choice, except to be killed (especially if the other vehicle was, say, a truck bearing down at full speed). Yet even in this case, the driver would be prosecuted and would have to plead their case in a court of law. Yet even in using this argument, I was regularly accused of making bad analogies and of being incapable of saying whether I, in the place of the killers and in an identical context, would not have done the same thing to save my own life. But in the end, the question is certainly not to know what I would have done—contrary to what Pierre Bayard says. This is unknowable. To paraphrase his title, though, it is very easy to ask the following question: "Would I have been judged innocent or guilty of my crimes?"

16. Sigmund Freud, "Thoughts for the Times on War and Death," in *The Standard Edition of the Complete Psychological Works of Sigmund Freud*, Volume XIV (1914–1916): *On the History of the Psycho-Analytic Movement, Papers on Metapsychology* (London: Hogarth Press, 1964).

17. Here Freud's thinking is no exception to the logic of dying for one's country. See Ernest H. Kantorowicz, *Mourir pour la Patrie et Autres Textes* (1951) (Paris: Fayard, 2004).

18. Victor Tausk, *Contribution à la Psychologie du Déserteur: Oeuvres Psychanalytiques* (1916) (Paris: Payot, 1975), 129–56. See also, Kurt Eissler, *Freud sur le Front de Névroses de Guerre* (Paris: PUF, 1992). For a more

detailed reading of the psychoanalytic controversies on the military stakes of war trauma, see José Brunner, "Will, Desire, and Experience: Etiology and Ideology in the German and Austrian Medical Discourse on War Neuroses, 1914–1922," *Transcultural Psychiatry* 37 (2000): 297–320, as well as Richard Rechtman, "Remarques sur le Destin de la Psychanalyse dans les Usages Sociaux du Traumatisme," *Revue Française de Psychosomatique* (2005): 27–38.

19. Karl Abraham, "Contribution à la Psychanalyse des Névroses de Guerre," in *Oeuvres Complètes*, vol. II (Paris: Payot, 1918), 173–80.

20. Sigmund Freud, "Why War?" (1933), in *The Standard Edition of the Complete Psychological Works of Sigmund Freud*, Vol. XXII (1932–1936), *New Introductory Lectures on Psycho-Analysis and Other Works* (London: Hogarth Press, 1964).

21. Freud, "Thoughts for the Times," 286.

22. Sigmund Freud, *Group Psychology and the Analysis of the Ego* (1921) (New York: Norton, 1990).

23. In a very summary fashion, let us recall that in the first of Freud's principles, the central hypothesis was founded on the existence of a "pleasure principle" toward which all unconscious desires converge. After 1920 and the introduction of the second principle, Freud held that a second principle, opposing but equally powerful, rivals the quest for pleasure. The death drive comes to figure for this desire for the destruction of the self or the other.

24. See the *Revue Française de la Psychanalyse* 80 (2016), dedicated to this text.

25. We should also note that Elias drew this idea from Freud but saw it through a positive lens that did not exist for Freud.

26. Freud, "Thoughts for the Times," 282.

27. See Freud's works on religion, such as *The Future of an Illusion* (1927) (New York: Norton, 1989). See also his writings on infant sexuality, in which he attempts to denounce the illusion of the absence of sexuality in childhood, in *Three Essays on the Theory of Sexuality* (1905) (New York: Verso, 2017).

28. Freud, "Thoughts for the Times," 285.

29. Freud makes no reference to the Armenian genocide, which was nevertheless already there as a demonstration of the atrocities that existed and could be reproduced. But at the time, the crime was still largely unknown or ignored or—worse—met with denial, especially in the German-speaking world that was still in alliance with Turkey.


### 3. ORDINARY MAN AND HIS PATHOLOGIES

1. Hannah Arendt, *The Life of the Mind* (New York: Harcourt, 1971), 3–4.

2. Hannah Arendt, *Eichmann in Jerusalem: A Report on the Banality of Evil* (New York: Viking, 1963).

3. See Michèle-Irène Brudny de Launay's excellent preface to *Eichmann à Jerusalem* (Paris: Folio, 2002).

4. Hannah Arendt, *The Origins of Totalitarianism* (New York: Schocken Books, 1951).

5. See Ivan Ermakoff, "Renoncement et Effondrement Politique," in *Politika: La Politique à l'Épreuve des Sciences Sociales* (https://www.politika.io/fr/notice /renoncement-effondrement-politique), 2017.

6. Arendt, *Eichmann*, 33.

7. Arendt, *Life of the Mind*, 4.

8. See Michel Foucault, *Abnormal: Lectures at the Collège de France, 1975–1975*, trans. Graham Burchell (New York: Picador, 2003). See also Marc Renneville, *Crime et Folie: Deux Siècles d'Enquêtes Médicales et Judiciares* (Paris: Fayard, 2003).

9. [I have retained the use of the term *génocidaire*—a person who commits mass murder of defenseless people under the authority of a state, army, or militant group of some sort—throughout the book. The French word is primarily (although not exclusively) used in English to refer to participants in the Rwandan genocide. In this book, it is especially important because it provides a way to discuss an individual's genocidal actions even outside of any genocide in the strictest sense of the term (see Chapter 4).—Trans.]

10. Arendt, *Eichmann*, 21–22.

11. Ibid., 25.

12. Bettina Stangneth, *Eichmann Before Jerusalem: The Unexamined Life of a Mass Murderer*, trans. Ruth Martin (New York: Vintage, 2015).

13. Arendt, *Eichmann*, 22.

14. Rithy Panh, *Duch: Master of the Forges of Hell* (New York: First Run Features, 2012), film. See also, Richard Rechtman, "Reconstitution de la scène du crime: À Propos de *Duch, le Maître des Forges de l'Enfer* de Rithy Panh," *Etudes* (July 2011): 320–39.

15. Christopher Browning, *Ordinary Men: Reserve Police Battalion 101 and the Final Solution in Poland* (New York: Harper Perennial, 1992).

16. Harald Welzer, *Les Exécuteurs: des Hommes Normaux aux Meurtriers de Masse* (Paris: Gallimard, 2007).

17. Daniel J. Goldhagen, *Hitler's Willing Executioners: Ordinary Germans and the Holocaust* (New York: Knopf, 1996).

18. Robert Jay Lifton, *Nazi Doctors: Medical Killing and the Psychology of Genocide* (New York: Basic Books, 1988), 48.

19. Elsewhere I have examined the harmful effects of contemporary ideas that posit that an exit from the species is nevertheless possible (for example, through the dehumanization or desubjectivation of men and women subject to the most extreme violence). Both in my clinical experience with direct survivors of processes of mass extermination or with victims of torture, and in the accounts I was able to collect during my surveys of political refugees, I have never encountered this famous "desubjectivation." The psychic consequences are, of course, often considerable, but it seems risky to me to call this desubjectivation. The proof of this

assertion, of course, deserves to be developed more fully but is outside the scope of my current remarks. I refer here to my previous research, especially "The Survivor Paradox: Psychological Consequences of the Khmer Rouge's Rhetoric of Extermination," *Anthropology & Medicine Journal* 13 (2006): 1–11; "L'Empreinte des Morts: Remarques sur l'Intentionnalité Génocidaire," in Phay-Vakalis, Soko (dir.), *Cambodge: l'Atelier de la Mémoire* (Paris / Phnom Penh, Sonluek Tmey / Centre Bophana / Université Paris 8, 2010); *Les Vivantes* (Paris: Léo Scheer, 2013); and "From an Ethnography of the Everyday to Writing Echoes of Suffering," *Medicine Anthropology Theory* 4 (2017): 130–42, https://doi.org/10.17157/mat.4.3.474.

20. Robert Antelme, *The Human Race*, trans. Jeffrey Haight and Anne Mahler (Evanston: Marlboro Press / Northwestern University Press, 1992).

21. Stanley Milgram, *Obedience to Authority: An Experimental View* (New York: Harper & Row, 1974).

22. Jonathan Littell, *The Kindly Ones*, trans. Charlotte Mandell (New York: HarperCollins, 2009). Charlotte Lacoste's work, previously cited, contains a remarkable deconstruction of this work and its (French) success.

23. François Bizot, *The Gate*, trans. Euan Cameron (New York: Knopf, 2003); *Facing the Torturer*, trans. Charlotte Mandell and Antoine Audouard (New York: Knopf, 2012).

24. See Sylvia Kerviel, "Mal Vus à la Télé," *Le Monde*, April 21, 2010, which offered the show's unfortunate participants a chance for "repentance."

25. See the chilling description of the everyday reality of Hutu genocide participants in Jean Hatzfeld, *Machete Season*, trans. Linda Coverdale (New York: Farrar, Straus, Giroux, 2006).

26. Didier Epelbaum, *Des Hommes Vraiment Ordinaires? Les Bourreaux Génocidaires* (Paris: Stock, 2015), Kindle position 142.

27. See, among others, Claudine Vidal, "Un Génocide à la Machete," in Marc Le Pape, Johanna Siméant, and Claudine Vidal (dir.), *Crises Extrêmes: Face aux Massacres, aux Guerres Civiles, et aux Génocides* (Paris: La Découverte, 2006), 21–35, as well as Hélène Dumas, *Le Génocide au Village: le Massacre des Tutsi de Rwanda* (Paris: Seuil, 2014).

28. Pierre Bayard, *Aurais-je été resistant ou bourreau* (Paris: Éditions de minuit, 2013).

29. See Daniel Zagury and Florence Assouline, *L'Énigme des Tueurs en Séries* (Paris: Plon, 2008), as well as Daniel Zagury, *La Barbarie des hommes ordinaires* (Paris: L'Observatoire, 2018).

30. Abram de Swaan, *Diviser pour tuer* (Paris: Seuil, 2016), 278.

31. Ibid., 278.

32. Itzhak Fried, "Syndrome E," *The Lancet* 350 (1997): 1845–47.

33. Psychological literature on the subject is extensive and in large part reproduces the same expectations and the same results. For a summary, see Robert Jay Lifton's *Nazi Doctors: Medical Killing and the Psychology of Genocide* (New York: Basic Books, 1988).

34. Norman Ohler, *Blitzed: Drugs in the Third Reich*, trans. Shaun Whiteside (New York: Houghton Mifflin Harcourt, 2017).

35. Laurent Laniel, "Captagon: Déconstruction d'un Mythe" (Paris: OFDT, 2017); Soren Seelow, "Captagon: Un Rapporte Démonte le Mythe de la 'Drogue des Djihadistes,'" *Le Monde*, July 27, 2017.

## 4. THE ADMINISTRATION OF DEATH

1. Herman Melville, *Bartleby, The Scrivener: A Story of Wall Street*, 1853.

2. See, for example, the almost surgical description given by Stéphane Audoin-Rouzeau in his *Quelle Histoire: Un Récit de Filiation (1914–2014)* (Paris: Hautes Études Gallimard / Seuil, 2013). See also Jesse Glenn Gray, *The Warriors: Reflections on Men in Battle* (New York: Harcourt, 1959).

3. See, for example, Manon Pignot, *L'Appel de la Guerre: Des Adolescents au Combat, 1914–1918* (Paris: Anamosa, 2019).

4. Michel Foucault, *An Introduction: Vol. 1 of The History of Sexuality*, trans. Robert Hurley (New York: Pantheon, 1978); *The Birth of Biopolitics: Lectures at the*

*Collège de France, 1878–1979*, trans. Graham Burchell (New York: Picador, 2010).

5. See the introductory chapter of *Discipline and Punish*, in which Foucault describes in minute detail the public torture of a classical age prisoner to demonstrate that what people came to see was not execution, cruelty, or even savagery but the visual expression of the sovereign's power. *Discipline and Punish: The Birth of the Prison*, trans. Alan Sheridan (New York: Pantheon, 1978).

6. Giorgio Agamben, *Homo Sacer: Sovereign Power and Bare Life*, trans. Daniel Heller-Roazen (Stanford: Stanford University Press, 1998).

7. Giorgio Agamben, *Remnants of Auschwitz: The Witness and the Archive*, trans. Daniel Heller-Roazen (New York: Zone Books, 2002).

8. Giorgio Agamben, *State of Exception*, trans. Kevin Attell (Chicago: University of Chicago Press, 2005).

9. The term "necropolitics," coined by Achille Mbembe (see *Necropolitics*, trans. Steven Corcoran [Durham: Duke University Press, 2019]), is also used to describe the management of human remains in the framework of post-genocide memorial politics: See Jean-Marc Dreyfus and Elisabeth Anstett, eds., *Human Remains in Society: Curation and Exhibition in the Aftermath of Genocide and Mass Violence* (Manchester: Manchester University Press, 2016).

10. These two elements make up the basis of Sémelin's argument contesting the use of the term "genocide" in

the case of the Khmer Rouge in Cambodia. Jacques Sémelin, *Purify and Destroy: The Political Uses of Massacre and Genocide*, trans. Cynthia Schoch (New York: Columbia University Press, 2007).

11. The ECCC's website lists all the investigations and arguments that have taken place during the trials, https://www.eccc.gov.kh/en.

12. ECCC, Summary of Judgment in Case 002-02, November 16, 2018, https://www.eccc.gov.kh/sites /default/files/media/20181217%20Summary%20of%20 Judgement%20Case%20002-02%20ENG_FINAL%20 FOR%20PUBLICATION.pdf.

13. Bruno Phillip, "Le Regime Khmer Rouge Jugé Coupable de Genocide," *Le Monde*, November 16, 2018. See also Adrien le Gal, "Cambodia: Pourquoi le Terme 'Geoncide' a Mis Quarante Ans à l'Imposer," *Le Monde*, November 16, 2018.

14. Noam Chomsky and Edward Herman, *Manufacturing Consent: The Political Economy of the Mass Media* (New York: Pantheon Books, 1988).

15. Without other proof, Chomsky and Herman advance that the Cambodian revolution did not cause more than 100 or 200 thousand deaths, much fewer than the American bombings (*sic*).

16. See Badiou's fiery editorial against Vietnamese intervention and for the glory of Pol Pot's regime. "Kampuchea Vancra," *Le Monde*, January 17, 1979.

17. Chomsky and Herman, *Manufacturing Consent*, 281.

18. Anonymous, "L'autopsie d'un Régime Génocid-aire: le Peuple Kampuchéen Juge Pol Pot et Iang Sary," *Bulletin de Vietnam*, supplement (51), 1979.

19. On the direct consequences of the Vietnamese intervention / invasion on the Cambodian people, see Esmerelda Luciolli, *Le Mur de Bambou: le Cambodge Après Pol Pot* (Paris: Régine Deforges / Médecins Sans Frontières, 1988).

20. "Hell" is indeed the term that most often occurred in the words and writings of Cambodian survivors when they spoke of the period.

21. Raphael Lemkin, "Genocide: A Modern Crime," *Free World* 9, no. 4 (April 1945): 39–43.

22. Resolution 260 A (111) of the United Nations General Assembly, December 9, 1948, entered into force January 12, 1951. See https://www.ohchr.org/EN /ProfessionalInterest/Pages/CrimeOfGenocide.aspx.

23. Jean Lacoutre makes an unfortunate use of the term several times to denounce the crimes he himself covered up during the regime's first years, when he was an ardent supporter of Pol Pot's revolution.

24. Georges Condominas, *L'Espace Social: À Propos de l'Asie du Sud-Est* (Paris: Flammarion, 1980).

25. Richard Rechtman, "Non ce ne Fut pas un Auto-Génocide," *Le Monde*, April 1998.

26. This comparison was the primary origin for the virulent polemic that the publication of the book produced, in which some of Courtois's coauthors (such as Nicolas Werth) distanced themselves from

his perspectives and from the general project of the work.

27. Courtois's definition is as follows: "Acts which, in the function of a concerted plan, attempt to destroy a social and/or political group as such, in whole or in part. If we adhere to the terms set by the 1948 convention, the first three—a, b, and c—were practiced to varying degrees by the Leninist regime between 1918 and 1922, by the Stalinist regime, and finally by the Khmer Rouge." "Le Génocide de Classe: Définition, Description, Comparaison," *Les Cahiers de la Shoah* 1 (2002): 89–122.

28. Klaus Hildebrand, "L'Ere des Tyrans," *Frankfurter Allgemeine Zeitung*, July 31, 1986.

29. See, for example, the brief account she dedicates to it at the beginning of Duch's trial, "Les Larmes de Douch," *L'Histoire*, April 2009.

30. We will see in what follows that this analysis must be seriously nuanced, because behind the goal of purifying the Cambodian Khmer, their planned extermination was objectively manifest.

31. Emphasis mine.

32. Khmer populations from the regions bordering south Vietnam and influenced by it.

33. Ben Kiernan, *The Pol Pot Regime: Race, Power, and Genocide in Cambodia, 1975–1979* (New Haven: Yale University Press, 1996), 3–4.

34. Jean-Marc Dreyfus and Elisabeth Anstett were among the first to contribute to making this question of the fate of millions of bodies destroyed in genocides

an essential component of research into mass atrocity. See Jean-Marc Dreyfus and Elisabeth Anstett, eds., *Destruction and Human Remains: Disposal and Concealment in Genocide and Mass Violence* (Manchester: Manchester University Press, 2014).

35. In his autobiography, Rithy Panh gives a chilling description of his work as "stretcher bearer" in a cooperative "hospital," which consisted of days spent carrying bodies. *The Elimination: A Survivor of the Khmer Rouge Confronts His Past and the Commandant of the Killing Fields* (with Christophe Bataille, trans. John Cullen) (New York: Other Press, 2012).

36. As attested to by the body of published survivor stories. See, for example, Ngor Haing, *Une Odyssée Cambodgienne* (Paris: Fixot, 1988); M. Szymusiak, *Les Pierres Crieront* (Paris: La Découverte, 1984); Ida Simon-Barouh and Yii Tan Kim Pho, *Le Cambodge des Khmers Rouges: Chronique de la Vie Quotidienne* (Paris: L'Harmattan, 1990).

37. We find a new version of this questioning in a recent essay by Klaus Theweleit, which posits that criminals are motivated by a form of transgressive *jouissance* that he connects to a liberating mechanism of psychic fragmentation of such passions. While this hypothesis could possibly be applied to the cases of isolated killers responsible for massacres in contemporary metropolitan centers that make headlines in the United States especially, but also in Norway after the recent acts of Anders Breivik, who brutally killed 77 young people

on the island of Utoya in 2011, it seems to me less credible to use it to take account of the psychic functioning of genocidaires. Once again, Theweleit's hypothesis rests mainly on the isolation of the killer's act and the construction that accounts for it. Conversely, though, if we take into consideration the whole of the process in which killing is only one element, then we can understand that *jouissance*, isolation, fragmentation, and the relative suspension of the conscience are improbable, given the time spent in organizing a quotidian reality in which death is always present. See Klaus Theweleit, *Le Rire des Bourreaux: Essai sur le Plaisir de Tuer* (Paris: Seuil, 2019).

38. I owe this meticulous analysis of the expanded topography of S-21 to Anne-Laure Porée, as part of her anthropology thesis in progress on S-21 at the EHESS. See also Anne-Laure Porée, "Tuol Sleng: L'Histoire Inachevée d'un Musée Mémoire," *Moussons: Recherche en Sciences Humaines Sur l'Asie du Sud-Est* 30 (2017): 153–83.

39. This is the reason for which it seems to me more useful to speak of "forms of life" than "lives" in the context of genocide, a point to which I will return in the following chapter.

## 5. THE ORDINARY LIFE OF GENOCIDAIRES

1. http://www.icty.org/fr/sp%C3%A9cial/aveux-de -culpabilit%C3%A9-0.

2. See the remarkable ethnographic work undertaken on the ICTY by Elisabeth Claverie, in "Démasquer la Guerre, Višegrad Avril–Juin 1992: Chronique d'un Nettoyage Ethnique," *L'homme* (2012): 204.

3. See Stanley Cavell, *This New Yet Unapproachable America: Lectures after Emerson after Wittgenstein* (Chicago: University of Chicago Press, 1988).

4. See Sandra Laugier, "Retour à la Vie Ordinaire: Introduction." *Raison Publique* 1 (2014): 9–17, as well as "L'ordinaire Transatlantique: De Concord à Chicago, en Passant par Oxford," *L'homme* 3/4 (2008): 169–99.

5. Joshua Oppenheimer's documentary *The Act of Killing* (2013) presents a notable exception to this rule.

6. Fernand Meyssonnier, *Paroles de Bourreau: Témoignage Unique d'un Exécuteur des Arrêts Criminels*, collected, introduced, and edited by Jean-Michel Bessette (Paris: Editions Imago, 2002), Kindle version.

7. Ibid., position 3155.

8. At least until the abolition of the death penalty in France, in September of 1981. See Frédéric Armand, *Les Bourreaux en France* (Paris: Perrin, 2012), Kindle version.

9. Meyssonnier, *Paroles de Bourreau*, position 2408.

10. Ibid., position 1778.

11. Ibid., position 1723.

12. "Yes, it bothered us to have to execute him. So my father said, 'we'll do it first.' I signaled to the two aides to let him go first, to spare him an awful wait." Ibid., position 2750.

13. "Yes, we made the guiltiest go last. It's been like that for centuries. But it's up to us. It's just what we can do as a favor to the condemned." Ibid., position 1878.

14. Ibid., position 1593.

15. Ibid., position 1786.

16. Ibid., position 1785.

17. Albert Ogein, "Les Formes de Vie d'un Point de Vue Sociologique," in Estelle Ferrase and Sandra Laugier, *Formes de Vie* (Paris: CNRS Editions, 2018): 127–47, 145.

18. Didier Fassin, *La Vie: Mode d'Emploi Critique* (Paris: Seuil, 2018).

19. Guillaume Le Blanc, *Vies Ordinaires, Vies Précaires* (Paris: Seuil, 2007).

20. Veena Das makes the neighborhood a fundamental element of ethnography. See her book *Affliction: Health, Disease, Poverty* (New York: Fordham University Press, 2015) as well as the essay "Companionable Thinking," *Medicine Anthropology Theory* 4 (2017): 191–203, https://doi.org/10.17157/mat.4.3.486.

21. See Richard Rechtman, "From an Ethnography of the Everyday to Writing Echoes of Suffering," *Medicine Anthropology Theory* 3 (2017): 130–42, https://doi.org/10.17157/mat.4.3.474.

22. See Sandra Laugier, "L'Ordinaire Transatlantique: de Concord à Chicago, en Passant par Oxford." *L'Homme* 3/4 (2008): 169–99.

23. Veena Das, *Affliction: Health, Disease, Poverty* (New York: Fordham University Press, 2015).

24. Hélène Dumas, *Le Génocide au Village: le Massacre des Tutsi du Rwanda* (Paris: Seuil, 2014).

25. Hélène Dumas, "Le Génocide des Voisins," *L'Histoire* 396:2 (2014): 48.

26. See the 2009 documentary by Anne Aghion, explicitly titled *My Neighbor, My Killer.*

27. Cyanne E. Loyle "Why Men Participate: A Review of Perpetrator Research on the Rwandan Genocide," *Journal of African Conflicts and Peace Studies* 1 (2009): 26–42.

28. See Chapter 3.

29. This accords with de Swaan's notion of compartmentalization, in *Diviser Pour Tuer* (2016).

30. See the interview conducted with a Hutu woman who attempted to kill her own son by Violaine Baraduc in her film *A Mots Couverts* (2015).

31. Jean Hatzfeld, *Machete Season*, trans. Linda Coverdale (New York: Farrar Straus Giroux, 2006).

32. Rob Lemkin and Thet Sambath, *Enemies of the People: A Personal Journey into the Heart of the Killing Fields* (Old Street Films, 2009), film.

33. Rithy Panh, *Graves Without a Name* (Catherine Dussart Productions and Anuheap Production, 2018), film.

34. Alexander Hinton, *Why Did They Kill: Cambodia in the Shadow of Genocide* (Oakland: University of California Press, 2004).

35. Lifton, in turn, writes a very positive preface to Hinton's book. For more on Lifton, see Chapter 3.

36. Andrej Umansky, *La Shoah à L'Est: Regards d'Allemands* (Paris: Fayard, 2018), Kindle version.

37. Ibid., position 12.

38. Ibid., position 16.

39. Ibid., position 28.

40. Ibid., position 52.

41. Ibid., position 53.

42. Ibid., position 146.

43. Ibid., position 252.

44. Ann Laura Stoler, *Along the Archival Grain: Epistemic Anxieties and Colonial Common Sense* (Princeton: Princeton University Press, 2009).

45. Richard Rechtman, "Altérité Suspecte et Identité Culpable Dans la Diaspora Cambodgienne," in Esther Benbassa and Jean-Christophe Attias, *La Haine Soi: Difficiles Identités* (Brussels: Complexe, 2006): 173–88.

46. Guillame Suon, *About My Father* (Phnom Penh: Bophana Productions, 2010), film.

47. Rob Lemkin and Thet Sambath, *Enemies of the People: A Personal Journey into the Heart of the Killing Fields*.

48. Ibid.

### CONCLUSION

1. As Freud often reminds us, even the most sadistic drives can be transformed into honorable acts, while the most noble unconscious intentions can produce the worst, as good can be imposed by force upon others.

2. Indeed, they are the foundation for the research into genocide and mass atrocity upon which my work depends.

3. See my work on the victims of the Khmer Rouge, in "From an Ethnography of the Everyday to Writing Echoes of Suffering," *Medicine Anthropology Theory* 4:3 (2017), 130–42, https://doi.org/110.17157/mat.17154.17153 .17474; *Les Vivantes* (Paris: Léo Scheer, 2013); "Archéologie Psychique de L'Intentionnalité Génocidaire: A propos du Cambodge des Khmers Rouges," in *Penser les genocides*, ed. Blandine Ghenton (Paris: Editions du CNRS, forthcoming 2021).

4. Aliza Luft, "Toward a Dynamic Theory of Action at the Micro Level of Genocide: Killing, Desistance, and Saving in 1994 Rwanda," *Sociological Theory* 33 (2015): 148–72.

5. See Richard Rechtman, "L'ambition Génocidaire de Daech," in *Résister à la Terreur*, ed. Nicolas Troung (Paris: L'Aube, 2016).

6. See Patrick Desbois, *The Holocaust by Bullets: A Priest's Journey to Uncover the Truth Behind the Murder of 1.5 Million Jews*, trans. Catherine Spencer (New York: Palgrave Macmillan, 2008). See also the Yahad-in-Unum site: https://www.yahadinunum.org.

7. Patrick Desbois and Natasie Costel, *La Fabrique des Terroristes* (Paris: Fayard, 2016).

8. See https://icty.org/en/features/statements-guilt.

9. Names have been changed.

10. The Dublin Accords called for asylum seekers arriving in Europe to make their demand for asylum in

the first country in which they arrived. This often means Hungary for those coming from Afghanistan, and Italy for Syrians and refugees from sub-Saharan Africa crossing the Mediterranean, most often from Libya—two countries in the EU whose strict politics with regards to migrants leaves them little chance. Even if they can move about Europe, the asylum seekers cannot claim asylum in another country and must wait for the first host country's response. As they have not yet gotten a response from the first country's administration, they can be expelled back to that country at any moment. At the end of several months of waiting, some seekers obtain the right to exit the Dublin rules and make a new demand in another country of their choice.

11. See Cécile Hennion, *Le Fil de Nos Vies Brisées* (Paris: Anne Carrière, 2019).

**Richard Rechtman** is an anthropologist and psychiatrist and director of studies at EHESS in Paris. Since 1990, he has directed a transcultural outpatient clinic for refugees in central Paris. He is the author of several books in French and coauthor, with Didier Fassin, of *The Empire of Trauma: An Inquiry into the Condition of Victimhood* (2009), which won the William A. Douglass Book Prize.

**Lindsay Turner**, a poet and translator, is Assistant Professor of English and Literary Arts at the University of Denver. She has translated books by Stéphane Bouquet, Souleymane Bachir Diagne, Anne Dufourmantelle, Frédéric Neyrat, and Ryoko Sekiguchi.

**Veena Das** is Krieger-Eisenhower Professor of Anthropology at the Johns Hopkins University.

## Thinking from Elsewhere

Robert Desjarlais, *The Blind Man: A Phantasmography*

Sarah Pinto, *The Doctor and Mrs. A.: Ethics and Counter-Ethics in an Indian Dream Analysis*

Veena Das, *Textures of the Ordinary: Doing Anthropology after Wittgenstein*

Clara Han, *Seeing Like a Child: Inheriting the Korean War*

Vaibhav Saria, *Hijras, Lovers, Brothers: Surviving Sex and Poverty in Rural India*

Richard Rechtman, *Living in Death: Genocide and Its Functionaries.* Translated by Lindsay Turner, Foreword by Veena Das

www.ingramcontent.com/pod-product-compliance
Lightning Source LLC
Chambersburg PA
CBHW032131020426
42334CB00016B/1115